Y0-AES-828

CAPITAL AND
EXPLOITATION

CAPITAL AND EXPLOITATION

BY JOHN WEEKS

PRINCETON UNIVERSITY PRESS
PRINCETON, NEW JERSEY

Copyright © 1981 by Princeton University Press

Published by Princeton University Press, Princeton, New Jersey

All Rights Reserved

Library of Congress Cataloging in Publication Data will be
found on the last printed page of this book

This book has been composed in Linotron Bembo

Clothbound editions of Princeton University Press books
are printed on acid-free paper, and binding materials are
chosen for strength and durability

Printed in the United States of America by Princeton
University Press, Princeton, New Jersey

FOR LIZ

CONTENTS

ACKNOWLEDGMENTS

Through the last decade and one-half, there has emerged a growing interest in Marxian theory. Why this should be the case is itself an interesting question in the process by which the material conditions of life in the industrial capitalist countries produce modes of thought and analysis of those conditions. Particularly in the United States, the influence of Marx on intellectuals and activists was slight until fifteen years ago. Indeed, the science of historical materialism ("Marxism") stayed alive as a subject in the United States primarily through the efforts of a few people: those associated with the journals *Monthly Review* and *Science and Society*, and individuals such as Paul Mattick and James Becker.

The student and black movements of the 1960s and early 1970s were largely atheoretical except on their fringes. I was involved in the antiwar movement and, in retrospect, cannot but be astonished how antitheoretical and even anti-Marxian that movement was. At one of the founding meetings of the Union of Radical Political Economists, in New York in 1968, Paul Sweezy addressed a group of young, radical economists and stated that to provide a radical critique of capitalism, one had to be a Marxist. It is doubtful that one in ten in the group agreed. Certainly I did not. It was only much later that I recognized the truth of Sweezy's statement and the debt which the present generation of American Marxists owe to him and others who held fast to that view through the repressive 1950s and antitheoretical, "radical" 1960s.

My own interest in Marxism began while teaching at Birkbeck College, University of London, in 1973-1975. Largely by happenstance, a group of economists collected there who subsequently have become well known to those familiar with the new Marxian literature: Ben Fine, Laurence Harris, and Susan Himmelweit. To these three I owe an intellectual debt, for their discussions of Marx excited me.

However, much more important in shifting my interest permanently from bourgeois economics to Marxian social theory was the influence of my wife, Elizabeth Dore. I first seriously read *Capital* at her insistence, and in our subsequent joint work most of the basic points of this book were developed. The book is dedicated to her, as it should be.

The manuscript came directly out of a two-term graduate course I taught at American University, and its progress roughly parallels the chronology of that course. Without the interaction of the exceptional group of political economy students at American University, the book probably would not have been written; in particular, I thank Louis Schorsch. While I was writing, Ben Fine was a visiting professor at American University and his help was invaluable; he even was willing to read chapters handwritten. His work is cited many times in what follows, and his influence goes beyond that.

Once the manuscript was completed, I was extremely fortunate to have publishers who sought excellent reviewers. Mike Williams (Brunel University), Laurence Harris (The Open University), Martin Fransman (University of Edinburgh), and James Becker (New York University), all provided suggestions and criticisms which, I think, improved the final draft. Also extremely helpful were the comments of Jeff Reiman of American University. In this context, I should also thank Sanford Thatcher of Princeton University Press and John Wallace of Edward Arnold for their aid. An excellent job of copyediting was done by Gail Filion of Princeton University Press, to whom particular thanks go.

Finally, particular thanks should go to Matthew and Rachel Dore-Weeks, who were considerate enough to time their birth a few days *after* I finished the manuscript.

CAPITAL AND EXPLOITATION

INTRODUCTION

In the *Communist Manifesto*, Marx and Engels state their famous dictum that, whereas previously analysts sought to explain the world, the purpose of their analysis is to change the world. And to change it in a particular way, i.e., to overthrow the rule of capital and establish a socialist society, itself merely a transitional phase to a communist society. Although Marx's ideas changed considerably between the publication of the *Manifesto* and the writing of his mature works, the central revolutionary purpose of his theoretical investigations remained unchanged.

In what follows, the theoretical core of Marx's critique of capitalism is presented to demonstrate that this critique, now over 100 years old, is also a critique of contemporary capitalism. The presentation is not an exercise in the history of thought, but rather an attempt to analyze the nature of contemporary capitalist society. My purpose is not to explain Marx's thought per se, but to explain capitalism. However, the basis of the explanation that follows can be found in the work of Marx, particularly the three volumes of *Capital*. Insofar as anyone except a student of the development of ideas should be interested in Marx's work, it is because that work explains the social world around him. And if this book makes Marx's writings more understandable, but provides no insight to capitalist society in the latter part of the twentieth century, it has failed in its purpose.

Anyone sampling the writings of those who identify themselves as Marxists quickly discovers that the term "Marxist" or "Marxian analysis" encompasses a wide variety of views, some of which are clearly in opposition. To some, these contradictory and frequently antagonistic interpretations indicate basic confusion within the structure of Marx's argument. While certainly there are points of internal confusion, the competing and conflicting interpretations (and outright rejections) of Marx's theory largely reflect the different political perspectives of those calling themselves "Marxists." Almost from the moment *Capital* was published, Marxists divided into two camps: those who, like Marx, concluded that capitalism could not be reformed to any basic degree and required violent overthrow by the working class and its political party; and those who thought that Marx's analysis could provide the basis for the reform and rationalization of capitalism, and a peaceful, even parliamentary transition to socialism. In the first decades of this century, these two camps were personified in V. I. Lenin, leader of the Russian Revolution, and Karl Kautsky, head of the German Social Democratic Party and former personal secretary to Friedrich Engels. The great debate between Lenin the revolutionary and Kautsky the reformer continues to rage among Marxist intellectuals and within the communist movement in each country of the world.

It is essential to realize at the outset that Marx's theory is not a critique of the *abuses* of capitalism. While *Capital* (particularly Volume I) is filled with contemporary examples of the horrors of the Industrial Revolution and capitalist abuses of the masses of the British population, Marx clearly considered capitalism to be progressive compared to previous social systems.[1] Marx's critique demonstrated that capitalism was (and is) but one historically specific mode of social reproduction, and one with its own inherent limits. The purpose of his theorizing (and the purpose of this book) was not to expose the abuses of capitalism, which were and are obvious to any observer, but to reveal the contradictory nature of capitalism, which necessarily sets limits to its development.

The key to unlocking the inner nature of capitalism is the labor theory of value. This theory, sometimes referred to as "the law of value," is not an aspect of the analysis of capitalism, but the theoretical core from which all other analysis unfolds. This view, that value theory is the theory of capi-

---

[1] The progressiveness of capitalism is discussed in Chapters II and III.

talist society, is reflected in the organization of this book. We begin with three chapters on value theory and its implications, in which it is demonstrated that the general production of useful objects ("use values," Marx called them) for exchange ("exchange values") necessarily implies a capitalist society, which is a society based on exploitation (the appropriation by the capitalist class of unpaid labor performed by the working class). These chapters demonstrate the central role in capitalist society of the process of value formation, the necessarily disruptive process by which technical changes generate uneven development among capitalist producers. This disruptive process manifests itself in the movement of relative prices. While capitalism is only one form of exploitative society, it is the only form in which the products of labor circulate in general in money form. The theory of money and credit (Chapters IV and V) unfolds from the theory of value, a logical extension of the contradictions arising from the process of value formation. This process of value formation, brought about by the movement of money capital, is a process of intraclass struggle, competition among capitals. The nature and inherent necessity of competition is demonstrated in Chapter VI. A consequence of competition (movement of capital) is technical change, what Marx called "the revolutionizing of the forces of production." This technical change is the central motive force of economic crises, giving rise to the famous "law of the tendency for the rate of profit to fall." The contradictory impact of technical change is explained in Chapter VII (on "fixed" capital), and brought together with the other elements of value theory (money, credit, and competition) in Chapter VIII, where economic crises are treated in detail.

The overall purpose of this unfolding of value theory is, as said, to explain the economic crises presently gripping the capitalist world. The intention is not merely to demonstrate the general tendency toward crises but also to account for their particular contemporary form. Capitalism is an inherently dynamic mode of social reproduction, and the forms its crises take change as capitalism matures. Thus, if value theory is generally valid, it must be able to account for concrete developments such as generally inflationary pressures, characteristic of capitalist economies since the 1960s, associated both with rapid accumulation and with depression and unemployment. The theory must also reveal the causes of international monetary instability and the failure of traditional Keynesian remedies to maintain domestic economic stability. In short, value theory has the task of explaining the concrete manifestations of capitalist crises throughout the capitalist epoch—depression, inflation, deflation, and "stagflation."

Placing value theory at the center of the analysis of capitalism is not common to all those who consider themselves Marxists. Contrary to this theoretical view is the work of Paul Baran and Paul Sweezy,[2] which explicitly rejects value theory as a tool of analysis. The Baran and Sweezy position has a large following in the English-speaking world: Howard Sherman, Erik Olin Wright, and Thomas Weisskoff are American representatives of this school. Others give some attention to value theory, but do not utilize it to explain crises and implicitly accept a secondary role for value theory. An example here would be Samir Amin, whose work is in French but extensively translated into English.

However, a growing group of writers recognizes the central role of value theory in the analysis of capitalism. This is particularly true in Europe, where the work of Ben Fine, Laurence Harris, Susan Himmelweit, Simon Mohun and Michel De Vroey generally complements the arguments of this book. In the United States, value theorists are still an emerging group, and the clearest example is Ira Gerstein; one should also include James Becker and Anwar Shaikh. These writers and this book have in common the view that value theory is the key to unlocking the inner nature of capitalism; that because of what Marx called "the fetishism of commodities," capitalism cannot be fruitfully analyzed in terms of its

[2] All the people referred to in this Introduction are discussed or cited subsequently; specific reference to their work is not given here.

surface manifestations (prices, profits, wages, etc.). Rather, these surface appearances hide the true nature of capitalist society and must be understood as reflections of the underlying value relations.

Historically, this recognition of the obfuscations of capitalism, that its operation creates illusions that cannot be taken at face value, is in the tradition of earlier Marxist writers such as Lenin, I. I. Ruben, and Henryck Grossman. This emphasis on the obfuscating nature of capitalist reproduction has been analyzed, often brilliantly, by the contemporary Italian Marxist Lucio Colletti.

In terms of Marx's work, the emphasis on value theory coincides with his "mature" writings—the *Grundrisse, Capital, Theories of Surplus Value*, and *A Contribution to the Critique of Political Economy*. Marx's analysis of capitalism developed and changed profoundly after 1848, when the course of political events in Europe drove him to devote his time largely to theoretical studies.[3] In all of these works, *value* plays a central, determinant role. In these mature works there are certainly inconsistencies, incomplete arguments and directly contradictory statements, though to a far less extent than Marx's critics would have one believe. What is consistent throughout is the central role of the law of value and its most important manifestation, the tendency of the rate of profit to fall. This interpretation of Marx's work, which is the basis of this book, can be called, for want of a better term, "orthodox" Marxism, a label that critics of capitalism should accept with pride. The pride does not come from a desire slavishly to repeat Marx, but from the recognition that the label refers to a particular method of analysis. In this method, value theory is employed to reveal the exploitation that the forms of capitalist reproduction obfuscate.

In the chapters that follow, the obfuscating nature of capitalist production will be a repeated theme. The obfuscations of capitalist society arise not from any conspiracy (though

[3] The course of Marx's career is analyzed in Martin Nicolaus's introduction to the *Grundrisse*.

certainly capitalists conspire in order to maintain their class rule), but from the nature of capitalist society itself, in which the class relations of that society appear as relations between commodities. We have now used the term "law of value" or "value theory" numerous times. In the most general sense, value theory is not primarily a theory of exchange or allocation, but a theory that reveals the class relations underlying a commodity-producing society.

Thus, as noted, our discussion must begin with an analysis of the value relation, the fundamental relation in capitalist society and the relation that is the *differentia specifica* of capitalism. In beginning this way, we immediately encounter the work of Marx's closest friend and repeated collaborator, Friedrich Engels. Engels was a towering figure in the world communist movement, a brilliant theoretician himself and responsible for the publication of Volumes II and III of *Capital*, which were left in various degrees of completion when Marx died. Every person who picks up either of the last two volumes of *Capital* owes a debt to Friedrich Engels.

Yet, as we shall see, Engels completely misconstrued Marx's value theory. It is Engels's presentation of the law of value that we use as our point of theoretical departure. It might seem a bit out of place to begin with a theoretical exposition from another century when our purpose is to demonstrate and elaborate the contemporary relevance of value theory. However, Engels's interpretation of Marx provides an excellent vehicle for establishing the historically specific nature of capitalist society. This insight is the basis for understanding the "laws of motion" of capitalist society, and these laws of motion show capitalism to be not only a historically specific mode of social reproduction but also a historically transitory one, in that its development is limited by those very laws.

Our discussion of the law of value provides the basis for developing a theory of economic crises. This method, developing crisis theory out of value theory, necessarily leads one through a discussion and analysis of money and credit (Chapters IV and V), competition (Chapter VI), and fixed capital (Chapter VII) before economic crises as such can be considered. Crisis theory arises out of the integration of all these elements, as the contradictions associated with each assert their concrete form through a break in the circulation of capital. Marxian writers who do not give central emphasis to value theory do not, in general, see the necessity to treat the topics dealt with in Chapters IV through VII, except in passing or as topics in their own right, largely divorced from the process of accumulation.

Crisis theories can, indeed, be formulated, however partially, without value theory. This is done by considering crises divorced from the production of commodities and emphasizing the circulation of commodities. Such theorists can be identified as "circulationists," and their theories take two forms: "underconsumptionism" and the "profit-squeeze" hypothesis. In the first view, which goes back at least as far as the French nineteenth-century radical Sismondi, economic crises ("depressions" or "recessions") are the consequence of inadequate aggregate demand. Such a crisis theory can be fully developed without any reference to Marxian analysis; indeed, John Maynard Keynes did precisely this. It is probably more correct to identify Marxists who hold to such a crisis theory as neo-Keynesians or radical Keynesians. Profit squeeze theorists similarly require no recourse to value theory, pegging their crisis theory to the wage-profit relationship in the tradition of Ricardo. According to these authors, crises result when accumulation reduces the size of the reserve army of the unemployed and wages are consequently forced up and profits down. This theoretical position is sometimes called the "class struggle" theory of crises, though this is a misnomer, for reasons elaborated elsewhere.[4] These two theories are in fact opposite sides of the same coin; for one, crises are the result of profits being too high, and, for the other, crises result from profits being too low. Surpris-

[4] See John Weeks, "The Process of Accumulation and the 'Profit Squeeze' Hypothesis," *Science and Society*, 43 (Fall 1979).

ingly, it is not beyond the wit of some writers to hold to both.

The argument of this book implies the rejection of both of these circulationist theories, though they are mentioned only in passing so as not to break the flow of the argument. Value theory is the heart of the analysis of capitalism, and value theory as presented in Chapters I through III implies a particular crisis theory. From one's crisis theory emerges one's view of the extent to which capitalism can be reformed. Thus, the final chapter here is not only a theoretical integration of previous elements but also a political statement of the historically transitory nature of the capitalist mode of production.

CHAPTER I

VALUE AS
EMBODIED LABOR

A. Introduction

The theory of value that Marx developed provides at the same time (1) the revelation that capitalism is merely one form of exploitative (class) society; (2) the explanation of the historical transition from precapitalist to capitalist society; (3) a theory of the concrete operation of a capitalist economy; and (4) an explanation of why others would explain the workings of a capitalist economy in an alternative theoretical framework. The theory explains not only current reality and how history gave rise to current reality but why erroneous theories of that reality exist. Without a clear grasp of the concept of value, such explanatory claim by a theory seems at best exaggerated, at worst metaphysical and vacuous—to explain everything is to explain nothing. Yet, the theory of value does provide the basis for all these analytical tasks. Capitalist society is the first society in which the reproduction of society and of the class relations of that society require the general circulation of commodities. This implies that the task of the theory of a capitalist society is to explain the integration of circulation and production, how socially isolated (private) production is rendered social. That is, how a social division of labor is affected without a conscious organization of social production. Within capitalist relations of production, this is obviously achieved through the exchange of products as commodities, and products not only are ex-

changed but must be exchanged.[1] Because of the central mediating role of exchange in capitalist society, the analysis of
the quantitative aspect of exchange necessarily must be considered. Indeed, it appears that this aspect of exchange's mediating role is the dominant one, since to individual producers the ratio in which their products exchange against other
products as commodities determines the conditions or even
the possibility of repeating the production and circulation
process.

While the quantitative aspect of exchange must be addressed and analyzed by any value theory, what distinguishes
Marx's value theory is that the quantitative aspect of exchange plays a minor role compared to the analysis of the
qualitative aspect, and the former derives from the latter. In
other words, the rate at which things exchange can only be
considered once one has a theory of why they exchange. The
two aspects are inseparable, and no "technical" explanation
of exchange exists divorced from the social relations that
govern exchange. While this relationship between the qualitative and quantitative aspects is basic to Marx's method and
to the understanding of the operation of a capitalist economy, it has been overlooked by generations of Marxian writers, and stressed infrequently. Therefore, any serious consideration of the labor theory of value must begin with a clear
formulation of what Marx called "the form of value" in order to avoid theoretical mistakes.

B. Engels's Formulation of the Theory of Value

The power of Marx's theory of value lies in its treatment of
the *form of value*, and this is the scientific basis of his consid-

---

[1] Marx summarizes this epoch-characterizing necessity by writing "the
character that [the producer's] own labor possesses of being socially useful
takes the form of the condition, that the product must be not only useful,
but useful for others, and the social character that his particular labor has of
being the equal of all other particular kinds of labor, takes the form that all
the physically different articles that are the products of labor, have one common quality, viz., that of having value." *Capital*, I, p. 78. All references to
Capital are to the Progress Publishers, editions 1970, 1967, and 1971 for
volumes I, II, and III, respectively.

eration of the magnitude of value. As many writers have pointed out, consideration of the latter without attention to the former characterizes the value theory of Ricardo, for example, and even more, of Sraffa and Sraffians.[2] Yet the treatment of the labor theory of value[3] as if it were merely a theory of the magnitude of value is common among those who consider themselves Marxists, and they can find support for their approach in an authority no less illustrious than Friedrich Engels.

Engels had a central role in the struggle to build the communist movement, and by doing so earned the respect of subsequent generations of revolutionaries. Engels was not merely Marx's friend and benefactor but also a revolutionary theorist of great importance. Recognition of Engels's contributions does not, however, require that his work be immune to criticism, and the following discussion, which demonstrates his basic disagreements with Marx, in no way implies that he did not make major contributions to the development of socialist thought and practice.

Engels appended to the end of Volume III of *Capital* a now-famous essay "Law of Value and Rate of Profit" in which he sought to answer Marx's critics by providing a brief explanation of his long-time collaborator's value theory. Because of the close association of Marx and Engels, this statement came to have major influence on the thinking of subsequent Marxists. A careful consideration of Engels's view is not merely an exercise in the history of thought, but can provide a full and clear understanding of the labor theory of value and, therefore, of the concrete operation of a capitalist economy.

In his defense of Marx, Engels begins by considering the

[2] On the difference between Ricardo and Marx, see Ira Gerstein, "Production, Circulation and Value," *Economy and Society* (August 1976); and on Marx and Sraffa, Susan Himmelweit and Simon Mohun, "The Anomalies of Capital," *Cambridge Journal of Economics* (Autumn 1978).

[3] Following Gerstein and Himmelweit and Mohun, I shall use the term "labor theory of value" to refer to the theory that analyzes the form of value, and "the labor-embodied theory of value" to refer to those theories that consider only the magnitude of value. The distinction will become clear below.

interpretation of Marx's theory of value by Sombart, a nine-teenth-century German economist who argued that value is not an empirical, but a mental construct.[4] That is, in a capitalist economy, value is not something of the real world, does not exist independently of one's conceiving it, but is a concept that one creates in order to explain reality. Engels agreed with this view[5] but objected that it was incomplete, that "it by no means exhausts the entire significance of the law of value for the economic stages of society's development dominated by the law."[6]

Engels then proceeds to argue that the law of value has ruled exchange for the entire history of the circulation of products as commodities: "the Marxian law of value holds generally, as far as economic laws are valid at all, for the whole period of simple commodity-production, that is, up to the time when the latter suffers a modification through the appearance of the capitalist form of production. . . . [T]hus the law of value has prevailed during a period of from five to seven thousand years."[7]

This is, indeed, a conclusion that leaps off the page at the reader (particularly since Engels's upper-limit estimate, seven thousand years, reaches back beyond recorded civilization). The assertion has two parts, which are closely related. First, that "the law of value holds generally" for all periods of commodity circulation. Second, that it holds *up to* the appearance of capitalism, when it undergoes a "modification." More important than the particular time span suggested by Engels is the fundamental view that the value form is not

[4] Friedrich Engels, "Law of Value and Rate of Profit," in *Capital*, III, pp. 817-818.

[5] Engels's comment is: "So says Sombart; it cannot be said that this conception of the significance of the law of value for the capitalist form of production is wrong." *Ibid.*, p. 894.

Morishima and Catephores state, "Engels rejected [Sombart's] interpretation immediately." But they refer to Sombart's implicit limitation of the law of value to capitalism. Michio Morishima and George Catephores, *Value, Exploitation and Growth* (N.Y.: McGraw-Hill, 1978), p. 179.

[6] *Capital*, III, p. 894.

[7] *Ibid.*, pp. 899-900.

specific to capitalism. Indeed, he suggests that it persists only in modified form under capitalism, and its pure form characterizes precapitalist society. These two related aspects of Engels's theory of value result from his method of analysis.

Engels develops his theory of the cause of exchange on the basis of a presupposed surplus of products arising in "more or less communistic communities."[8] It is unclear if this surplus is a general surplus over subsistence production or particular surpluses of specific use values. The ambiguity is important, for the former implies a class society, since a general surplus can exist as an objective phenomenon only if it is appropriated from the direct producer. In the absence of specific reference to classes, there can be no analysis of the appropriation of the surplus product from a producing class to a nonproducing class. Without classes, no part of society's production appears as a surplus. In such circumstances, a surplus product must be deduced on the basis of some physical (subsistence) definition of surplus, which the analyst necessarily imposes externally upon the society. Thus, a general surplus product either is an objective phenomenon of exploitation, an observable, material fact of society; or it becomes arbitrarily and subjectively defined by an external observer. On the other hand, if Engels is not referring to a general surplus, but to surpluses of specific products (use values), then he necessarily implies a division of labor, such that the surpluses reflect the producers' anticipation of being able to exchange one use value for another. In other words, a process is presupposed by which individual producers or groups of producers have decided to specialize to some degree. In either case, we have a presupposition of certain social relations upon which exchange is predicated, a point pursued in detail in the following section.

On the basis of these surpluses, exchange develops between communities first, "but later also prevails within the community."[9] Thus the explanation of exchange is based on

[8] *Ibid.*, p. 895.
[9] *Ibid.*

the existence of individual productivity or specialization. Further, this exchange generates the dissolution of these primitive communities, so that the circulation of the products of labor is seen as the motive force for changes in social relations among producers. The exchange is carried out by "family heads," who have the right to the product of their labor.[10] As the argument develops, we begin to get a picture of the society being considered, which presumably endured for five to seven thousand years: a society of independent, exchanging producers ("working peasants . . . with . . . their own farmsteads"), specializing within a social division of labor, and with property rights to the entire product of their labor. It is unclear how such a society allows for exploitation and classes, since the basis of class society is the appropriation of the surplus product of the direct producers, but this anticipates the critique of Engels's argument.

This exchange is explicitly treated as marginal to the reproduction of the producing families ("the little that such a family had to obtain by barter or buy"),[11] and the method of manufacture of the products obtained in exchange is presumed to be known by the exchanging families, i.e., not just by the producer of each product. At this point Engels gives an explanation for the division of labor that the exchange process presupposes: "[Exchange] consisted principally of the objects of handicraft production, that is, such things the nature of whose manufacture was by no means unknown to the peasant, and which he did not produce only because he lacked the raw material or because the purchased article was much better or very much cheaper."[12]

This implies that specialization—division of labor—derives from some process akin to "comparative advantage"; choice of what to produce is an individually determined one based on resource endowments and abilities. Explicit here is a view that those in the exchange process meet each other in the marketplace as equals—"the peasants, as well as the people

[10] *Ibid.*
[11] *Ibid.*, p. 897.
[12] *Ibid.*

from whom they bought, were themselves workers; the exchanged products were each one's own products."[13] We must
keep in mind that Engels is not describing a class society in
which the surplus products are appropriated and exchanged
by the ruling class, but a society of equals, exchanging the
products of their labor.

The analysis of the magnitude of value follows directly
from this analysis of social relations.

> Hence the peasant of the Middle Ages knew fairly ac-
> curately the labor time required for the manufacture of
> the article obtained by him in barter. What had they
> expended in making these products? Labor and labor
> alone. . . . [H]ow then could they exchange these prod-
> ucts of theirs for those of other laboring producers
> otherwise than *in the ratio of the labor expended on them*?
> Not only was the labor-time spent on these products the
> only suitable measure for the quantitative determination
> of the values to be exchanged; no other was possible.[14]

The argument for the quantitative determination of exchange is clinched by Engels with a rhetorical question ap-
pealing to the native intelligence of the peasant and crafts-
man, "Or is it believed that the peasant and the artisan were
so stupid as to give up the product of ten hours labor of one
person for that of a single hour's labor of another?"[15]

We can summarize Engels's theory of value as follows:
exchange occurs because of the production of a technologi-
cally available surplus and specialization that is prompted by
producers achieving quality or cost advantages based on ac-
cess to raw materials or individual abilities; the magnitude of
value is determined by the knowledge or perception by the

---

[13] *Ibid.*

[14] *Ibid.*

[15] This concluding question is buttressed by the assertion, "[N]ot only
does the peasant know the artisan's working conditions, but the latter
knows those of the peasant as well . . . People in the Middle Ages were
thus able to check up with considerable accuracy on each other's production
costs . . . at least in respect of articles of daily general use." *Ibid.*

exchanging parties of the labor time required in production; and this knowledge is obtained from direct observation. Further, this system of exchange is based upon each independent producer possessing the right to the full product of his labor.

Engels then argues that such a theory necessarily implies that the law of value so stated undergoes a major modification with the introduction of money ("metallic money" is Engels's term); indeed, that this law of value operates in its purest form when exchanges are barter.[16] With the introduction of a money commodity, "value" in the sense Engels uses the term becomes obscured. The obfuscation is of a particular type; namely, that which before was directly perceived—at least according to the argument—can no longer be perceived; to wit, with the introduction of money, "[T]he peasant and artisan were partly unable to estimate approximately the labor employed therein. . . . From the practical point of view, money became the decisive measure of value. . . . [T]he more [commodities] came from distant countries, and the less, therefore, the labor-time necessary for their production could be checked."[17]

Our purpose at the moment is to provide a faithful rendering of Engels's theory. However, one cannot help but note that it is not obvious why money should play an obfuscating role. If peasants and artisans have direct knowledge of the concrete labor time expended in production of commodities, and exchange is based on this knowledge, the introduction of money merely requires the seller to keep in mind how much of his labor time is exchanged against a given quantity of the money commodity when he becomes a buyer of a commodity whose embodied labor time he knows. In other words, if labor times are known, they are known whether exchanges involve money or not.[18] Engels deals

[16] Engels refers to "this barter on the basis of quantity of labor." *Ibid.*, p. 898.

[17] *Ibid.*, p. 899.

[18] And the labor time embodied in money is irrelevant to the exchange. If it is known, then money is no different from any other commodity in the theory. If unknown, this ignorance only affects the producer and exchanger of money, not those who exchange other commodities via money.

with this inconsistency by saying, "[C]onsciousness [on the part of peasants and artisans] of the value-measuring property of labor had been fairly well dimmed by the habit of reckoning with money; in the popular mind money began to represent absolute value."[19]

Whether or not one thinks that consciousness and habit play a decisive role in the quantitative determination of exchange, this position would seem to be inconsistent with Engels's rhetorical question about the intelligence of peasants and artisans. One could ask, "is it believed that the peasant and artisan, having direct knowledge of embodied labor times, were so stupid as to forget this knowledge with the introduction of money?" Given that the theory is based on perception, the key to the obfuscation of embodied labor time would have to be the fact that commodities begin to come "from distant countries," so that embodied labor cannot be directly known. Money in such a theory plays no role except as a convenient unit of account; it is merely a means of circulation.[20] Its use in exchange does not affect Engels's theory so long as exchange is between individual direct producers, his comments to the contrary notwithstanding.[21]

Once Engels has presented his theory of value, which is explicitly formulated for noncapitalist relations of production, he considers the transition to capitalism and the relevance of value, as he has defined it, for that mode of production. Once capitalist relations are considered, one must establish a theory of profit. On this point, he begins with merchant's capital, a form of capital that pre-dates industrial capital and the appropriation of surplus value. Here his ar-

---

[19] Ibid.

[20] The theory of money and the money form is considered in Chapter IV, after we have dealt with the value form.

[21] Ibid., p. 899. In fact, elsewhere Engels seems to argue this: "the introduction of metallic money brought into operation a series of laws which remain valid for all countries and historical epochs in which metallic money is a medium of exchange." Friedrich Engels, Anti-Duhring (Peking: Foreign Languages Press, 1976), p. 187.

Since metallic money appeared in antiquity, its "series of laws" must have prevailed for several thousand years, co-existent with the exchange Engels analyzes. The only function of money mentioned is as means of circulation.

gument parallels his earlier one. Merchants, like artisans and peasants, know each others' costs, and on the basis of these perceptions, "the merchant's efforts are deliberately and consciously aimed at making this rate of profit equal for all participants."[22] Thus, in precapitalist times, not only did products exchange as commodities according to embodied labor time but there was a tendency for rates of profit on merchant capital to equalize.[23] Both of these tendencies were the result of direct knowledge and perception of labor times and costs.

It should be noted that the existence of merchant's profit contradicts exchange at embodied labor time. Since by definition merchant's capital exists only in circulation ("pinned in circulation" Marx says), profit must arise from unequal exchange—buying below value and selling above value. Engels points this out and observes that the precapitalist world was characterized by equal exchange domestically (between individual producers) and unequal exchange internationally (under merchant's capital). In this context he makes the observation that the opposite holds in the "present-day world."[24] So we have the suggestion of a fundamental difference between capitalist and precapitalist exchange based on the geographical character of that exchange. It thus appears that the law of value developed by Engels cannot abstract from the spatial dimension of exchange.

From this theory of value derives a particular view of the transition to capitalism. The view Engels presents in his essay at the end of Volume III of *Capital* is substantially the same as that in *Anti-Duhring*, where he summarizes his analysis by writing, "The entire process [of the development of capitalism] is explained by *purely economic* causes, without the necessity for recourse *even in a single* instance to robbery, the state, or political interference *of any kind*."[25]

In Engels's view, whereas the transition may have involved force, we can understand it by abstracting from force,

[22] *Ibid.*, pp. 901-902.
[23] "[T]his high rate of profit, equal for all participants." *Ibid.*, p. 902.
[24] *Ibid.*
[25] Engels, *Anti-Duhring*, p. 208. Emphasis added.

the state, etc., "political influence of any kind," and considering it in purely economic terms. Since the development of capitalism involves the separation of labor from the means of production, it must be the case that this separation itself can be explained by purely economic causes with no necessary recourse to force.[26] In specific, the precapitalist society in which Engels's law of value operates is one in which rural and urban producers have control or ownership of their tools and land (in the case of farmers). Such an arrangement cannot be the basis of capitalist production, since under capitalist production relations it is the capitalist who monopolizes the means of production, with the result that the mass of the laboring population must of necessity hire itself out to the capitalist. Engels, then, hypothesizes that this basic change is achieved essentially without force. This is consistent with his view that it is exchange that generates changes in social relations, noted above.

Engels then explains how the transition to capitalism occurred by asking another rhetorical question: "Now what could induce the merchant to take on the extra business of a contractor?";[27] that is, to organize and control the production process. Thus, the explanation of the transition is situated at the individual level. The epochal dissolution of feudal relations, the separation of labor from the means of production, will be explained by the motivations of individuals. By taking this approach, Engels anticipates the argument of Sweezy in the debate over the transition to capitalism that developed in the 1950s.[28]

The answer to the question is obvious: only the anticipation of an increased profit would induce the merchant to be-

[26] In *Anti-Duhring*, Engels argues that capitalist private property emerges "in the interest of increased production and of the furtherance of trade—hence as a result of economic causes."

[27] *Capital*, III, p. 905.

[28] Rodney Hilton, ed., *The Transition From Feudalism to Capitalism* (London: New Left Books, 1976). Sweezy argues that landlords switched to wage labor in response to the spread of exchange, since this form of exploiting labor proved more profitable.

come a "contractor."[29] The question arises, however, as to the source of this increased profit. Since the artisan is assumed to have the right to the full product of his labor, no increased profit can be made without a change in the social relations of production. In other words, somehow the merchant must effect an appropriation of part of the product of the artisan's labor. Engels considers that the artisan willingly, voluntarily accepts the exploitation that profit making requires, "By thus *guaranteeing the weaver regular employment*, [the merchants] could depress the weaver's wage to such a degree that a part of the labor-time furnished remained unpaid for."[30]

Thus the transition from individual private property in the product of labor, with the artisan owning his own means of production, to capitalist exploitation and the separation of labor from the means of labor is achieved through a voluntary agreement, a sort of social contract in which one group chooses wage slavery and the other group greater profit. Further, wage employment is assumed to involve a guarantee of regular employment compared to the situation of self-employment. This would seem to be a somewhat controversial assessment of the stability of capitalist employment. Engels attempts to give verisimilitude to this theory of the transition to capitalism with a numerical example involving "the certainly very modest surplus value rate of 25 percent."[31] Once this voluntary pact between exploited and exploiter is put into operation, the "merchant-contractor" is able to undersell his competitors, and these "will also gradually be converted into contractors," presumably by their seeking out more artisans willing to trade part of their product for regular employment. As this process develops, we embark upon the epoch of the production of surplus value. The main motive force for this development is the advance of the productive forces associated with large-scale industry, which renders the remaining craftsmen, who stubbornly refuse to treat

[29] *Capital*, III, p. 905.
[30] *Ibid.*, emphasis added.
[31] *Ibid.*

with the merchants-cum-contractor, unviable because of higher costs.

Engels establishes his theory of the rate of profit in capitalist production without ever employing the concept of value of labor power (valorized necessary labor time). For him, profit arises purely from a change in the distribution of the net product of labor, and the precise rate of surplus value is determined at the outset separately in each production unit, depending upon the bargain struck between exploiter and exploited.

We can briefly summarize Engels's view of the transition to capitalism: it is a purely economic process, induced by the prospect of higher profit, with merchant capitalists becoming contractors; the profit is obtained through a largely voluntary agreement of artisans to surrender their independent status and accept lower "wages," implying that profit arises in distribution, not production; and finally, the process is generalized by the development of the productive forces, which makes capitalistically produced commodities progressively cheaper.

C. MEEK'S VIEW OF VALUE
BEFORE CAPITALIST RELATIONS

For those who feel that the concept of value should not have as its theoretical basis the *perception* by individuals, Ronald Meek provides an alternative interpretation that maintains the spirit of Engels's general outlook. Meek's analysis seeks to demonstrate the regulating role of value on an objective basis, rather than upon the subjective (perception).[32] Like Engels, Meek argues that Marx's value analysis applies to a range of "commodity producing systems," and capitalism must be visualized "first and foremost as a *particular form of the system of commodity production.*"[33]

Meek's argument is that Marx must have believed that

[32] Ronald Meek, *Smith, Marx and After* (London: Chapman and Hall, 1977).

[33] *Ibid.*, p. 128.

value ruled exchange before capitalism, since he (Marx) spends much of Volume I of *Capital* considering the exchange of commodities at their embodied labor times. Since we know that commodities do not exchange in such proportions under capitalist relations,[34] why else would Marx begin with exchange under such a rule unless he thought it had actually occurred historically? In short, Meek thinks that commodities exchanged at value before capitalism, then ("the morning after") exchange at prices of production after capitalism develops. By "prices of production" is meant exchange values that tend to equalize the rate of profit across industries (see Chapter III).

> Marx's *logical* analysis of commodities, money, and value, I believe, and in particular his analysis of the transformation of values into prices, *was* envisaged by him as a kind of "corrected reflection" of a real development which had taken place in history. . . .
>
> In its "classical form" as Marx conceived it, simple or petty production is a state of affairs . . . in which a significant minority of products is produced as commodities, under fairly competitive conditions, by independent artisans and peasants who own their own means of production and who therefore think of their net receipts as a reward for their labor.[35]

Meek's position is quite close to Engels's: both postulate a precapitalistic society of independent producers united with their means of production, exchanging their products according to embodied labor time. However, in Meek's view, this exchange is quantitatively achieved not by knowledge or perception, but by competition. When critics argued that

---

[34] This is because the movement of capital tends to equalize the rate of profit. Thus relevant for capitalism at the level of analysis of many capitals are "modified values." See Gerstein, "Production, Circulation and Value." Marx considers these "modified values" ("prices of production") in the first part of Vol. III of *Capital*.

[35] *Capital*, p. 143.

Meek's system implied competition, he conceded this and sought to establish historical evidence for it.[36]

In fact, Engels's argument implies competition among producers, even if he does not argue this explicitly. Knowledge of embodied labor time is useful only if it can be acted upon, Morishima and Catephores point out; if, for example, urban artisans produce within guilds that control membership and output levels, then monopoly pricing by the guilds could force peasants to accept exchange ratios above those implied by embodied labor times. These authors conclude that mobility of persons between crafts and occupations is a necessary condition to equalize rates of remuneration per unit of labor time.[37] In other words, exchange at any moment would be determined by supply and demand. If there were excess demand for a commodity, attempts by the buyer to obtain it at its embodied labor time either would be unsuccessful or leave some buyers unsatisfied, which would eventually push up the market price of the commodity, and it would no longer exchange at its embodied labor time. A barter in which a peasant surrendered, say, "ten hours of labor time for a single hour's labor of another" (to use Engels's example) would reflect not stupidity, but market conditions and the fact that all market exchanges occur between individuals in the context of *many* buyers and sellers.

Thus Meek's competitive mechanism would seem a necessary component of Engels's theory of value. We can summarize the amended analysis as follows: prior to the capitalist epoch, there existed for a considerable period of time societies of commodity producers who had right to the product of their labor; exchange in such societies tended to be at embodied labor times, and this rule of exchange was generated by competition among producers, including mobility between occupations.

---

[36] M. Morishima and G. Catephores, "Is There a 'Historical Transformation Problem'?" *Economic Journal*, 85 (1975), and Meek's reply. The critique is also found as Chapter 7 of Michio Morishima and George Catephores, *Value, Exploitation and Growth*. We consider their critique below.

[37] Morishima and Catephores, *Value, Exploitation and Growth*, p. 184.

D. Engels's Theory in Relation to Marx's

An introduction to Engels's *On Marx's Capital* published under the auspices of the Institute of Marxism-Leninism of the Soviet Union contains an assessment of the essay by Engels that we have summarized above, "Engels's essay is a splendid model of genuine materialist explanation of the Marxian theory of value; and is still unsurpassed as a weapon in the fight against all kinds of idealist distortions of Marxism."[38]

In the following chapter, we shall show that such an assessment is incorrect. The entire thrust, as well as the intricate detail of Marx's mature work is contrary to Engels's view.[39] In these works, Marx contradicts, refutes, and wages polemical attacks against precisely the views presented in "Law of Value and Rate of Profit." Our primary purpose in what follows is to develop the central theoretical concepts that reveal the operations of a capitalist economy and that allow a scientific understanding of its concrete operation. With such a purpose, it is of secondary interest which particular person was correct. However, because of Engels's great stature among Marxists, it is impossible to avoid direct criticism of his work, particularly since his essay provides an almost heuristic vehicle for demonstrating what is incorrect. To avoid a presentation that appears as an exercise in the history of thought for its own sake, demonstration of Marx's opposition to Engels's views is set off in an appendix. This allows the central thrust of the discussion to be a development of the value concept, rather than "Marx's value concept." However, in the appendix it is demonstrated, "beyond a shadow of doubt," that Marx's and Engels's views were opposed.

[38] "Forword," in Friedrich Engels, *On Marx's Capital* (Moscow: Progress Publishers, 1972), p. 9, where "Law of Value and Rate of Profit" is reprinted.

[39] Here we refer to *A Contribution to the Critique of Political Economy, Grundrisse, Capital,* and *Theories of Surplus Values.*

CHAPTER II

VALUE AS
A SOCIAL RELATION

A. CONCRETE AND ABSTRACT LABOR

The method of Engels, which is common to modern neo-Ricardians and Sraffians, is to move immediately from concrete labor to value-creating labor; or, in other words, from the use value of labor immediately to exchange value. The twofold nature of labor and labor power is ignored in this approach. In a famous letter, Marx gave what he considered "the two best points in my book" (*Capital*), and the first he lists is the dual and contradictory nature of value-creating labor power.[1]

The significance of this insight can be demonstrated by considering the exchange of two commodities. As use values, they are by nature noncomparable, possessing different objective characteristics. It is as values that they exchange, in which their useful character is abstracted. The problem of their noncomparability as use values is not resolved analytically by treating them as products of human labor. Just as the use values themselves are qualitatively different, so are the labors that produce them. The work of a carpenter is qualitatively different from that of a farmer, just as a chair is different from an ear of corn. The physical fact that each expenditure of effort occurs in the dimension of time no more indicates the exchange value of the commodities than the fact that both occupy a certain amount of three dimensional space. Marx makes this point clearly, "Because trade may, for example, consist in the exchange of the labor of a

[1] Karl Marx and Friedrich Engels, *Selected Correspondence* (Moscow: Progress Publishers, 1965), p. 192.

shoemaker, miner, spinner, painter and so on, is therefore the labor of the painter the best measure of the value of shoes?"[2]

The mistake is obvious if one asks, can the square footage of painted walls be the measure of the value of shoes? Clearly it cannot be, for some mediating form is required whereby that which is common to the use values (and concrete labor) becomes manifest. It is contrary to the laws of physics that a painted wall be directly transubstantiated into a number of shoes; concrete labor is not directly reducible to exchange value, as Engels would have it. Marx could have been commenting upon "Law of Value and Rate of Profit" when he wrote, "Boisguillebert's work proves that it is possible to regard labor-time as the measure of the value of commodities, while confusing the labor which is materialized in the exchange value of commodities and measured in time units with the direct physical activity of individuals."[3]

As our argument unfolds, we will show that value in the scientific sense is unobservable directly and that knowledge or perception of labor time is in any case irrelevant to the determination of exchange values. Be this as it may, if one does know the time a shoemaker spends making a shoe, this provides no additional information for determining the exchange value of the shoes than knowing it is, in fact, shoes that are being made.

Just as the distinction between abstract and concrete labor allows one to see the mistake of Engels's stress on perception of labor time, it also will, by a more involved process of argument, reveal that Meek is incorrect in arguing that competition among independent producers who own their own means of production results in exchanges at value. It will become clear that value systematically rules exchange only under capitalist relations of production and in no other system, historical or hypothetical.

    [2] Karl Marx, A Contribution to the Critique of Political Economy (Moscow: Progress Publishers, 1970), p. 56.
    [3] Ibid., p. 54.

B. Private Labor and Social Labor

Engels and others before and after him took the quantitative aspect of exchange as the problem posed for solution.[4] Yet the actual problem is much broader: how do we analyze a society characterized by the general production and circulation of the products of labor as commodities? Given this, one must decide at what historical juncture the analysis is to begin, since exchange, and exchange with money, is thousands of years old (as Engels points out). It is obvious that commodity circulation reaches its most developed stage under capitalism, both quantitatively (the extent of the valorization of the productions of labor) and qualitatively (the complexity of production and circulation). If we view a system in its most developed form, we can observe tendencies and characteristics that were latent at earlier stages. For this reason, the commodity and its implications are revealed by viewing it in the context of capitalism. Thus, the intention to explain commodity circulation and to reveal the laws of motion of capitalist society coincide analytically.

The central characteristic of the capitalist mode of production, a characteristic from which all others follow, is that the private labor of individuals is not directly social, but must be rendered social by the exchange of products as commodities. By directly social labor, we mean labor performed within social relations in which the particular concrete labor carried out by individuals is consciously assigned by the social unit, which by definition implies also that the products created are also consciously determined at the same time, and that these products are distributed as use values, not through exchange. In all societies individuals labor, but within capitalist relations of production this labor is carried out in production units that are socially isolated. No division of labor is estab-

---

[4] Marx comments as follows on this, referring to one of the United States of America's founding fathers: "From the outset Franklin regards labor-time from a restricted economic standpoint as the measure of value. The transformation of actual products into exchange-values is taken for granted, and it is therefore only a question of discovering a measure of their value." *Ibid.*, p. 56.

lished by custom or central authority prior to production. Producers discover through the exchange of their products whether their individual production decisions conform to the requirement that society as a whole be reproduced in an adequate manner. In some manner, via the interaction of commodity producers, private labor must be integrated into a socially cohesive whole. The labor theory of value is the analysis of how private labor becomes socialized and explains this process through an analysis of how concrete, specific labor is rendered abstract.[5]

In capitalist society, the relations of production dictate specific laws of exchange. In this mode of production, the direct producer has been separated from the means of production and can only be reunited with them via exchange—by the capitalist advancing capital in money form for labor power and the means of production.

To understand this, we must first consider the manner in which concrete labor is rendered abstract. In a society of commodity producers, concrete labor is expended in the labor process. This concrete expenditure of labor power provides the material basis for the circulation of commodities, since only that which is produced can be exchanged. However, different commodity producers may expend different quantities of labor time in the production of the same product, so that even in one branch of industry exchange need not imply a standard or normal expenditure of concrete labor time in production. At this point in the analysis, exchange merely renders all labor times commensurate, comparable: we do not yet have a theory to explain why there should be a tendency for producers of the same commodity to produce with equal efficiency.[6] Obviously, it is the social interaction

---

[5] In Rubin's words, "Productivity of labor—abstract labor—value—distribution of social labor: this is the scheme of a commodity economy in which value plays the role of regulator." I. I. Rubin, *Essays on Marx's Theory of Value* (Detroit: Black and Red, n.d.), p. 67. The same schema is used in Gerstein, "Production, Circulation and Value," *Economy and Society* (August 1976).

[6] Karl Marx and Friedrich Engels, *Collected Works* (New York: International Publishers, 1976), VI, pp. 126ff., where Marx comments upon Proudhon's embodied labor theory of value.

of producers as commodity producers (competition) that establishes this norm. But competition itself is insufficient to do so; it must be competition *within certain relations of production.*

Consider first the case of individual producers who own their own means of production and take the extreme case where none of the inputs used in production is bought, but all are produced within a self-contained labor process (such as a subsistence farmer selling a portion of his product). In this case, only the final product of the labor process is a commodity. Each article of the means of production is produced in social isolation by each producer, never facing the discipline of competition. There is no social mechanism for bringing about a normal expenditure of labor time in the products that are the means of production. In such a situation, competition's only function is to impose the rule of a uniform selling price in the market place. Here, price is a "merely formal moment for the exchange of use values."[7]

This hypothetical situation involves essentially noncommodity production, in that exchange does not appear until the end of the process, when all aspects of the labor process have already been determined independently of exchange. Because the means of production are not exchanged, the producer faces no objective necessity to expend any particular amount of labor time on them. The only objective necessity is that his or her total labor expenditure (and that of the family) on use values produced, exchanged and not exchanged, be sufficient to allow for the reproduction of the family. Should some producers be able to deliver their commodities with less expenditure of effort than others, the more "efficient" producers will enjoy a higher standard of

[7] "To the extent that money mediates this exchange the determination of prices will become important on both sides, but it will do so for [the buyer] only so far as he does not want to pay too much for the *use value* of labor; not in so far as he is concerned with its value [emphasis added]. The essence of the relation remains unchanged even if this price which begins as conventional and traditional is thereafter increasingly determined economically; . . . nothing is essentially changed thereby, because the determination of prices remains a *merely formal moment* for the exchange of mere use values." K. Marx, *Grundrisse* (New York: Vintage, 1973), p. 467.

living. This higher standard of living of some in no way pressures the less efficient to raise their efficiency. Indeed, as envious as they may be, the differences in concrete labor time expended may be beyond the ability of producers to change, due to differences in soil fertility, size of family, etc.

There is a more profound point to be made, which casts doubt upon the very validity of comparing concrete labor times in this hypothetical case. Since inputs are not exchanged, there is no real distinction in the process of the reproduction of the family between labor performed for exchange and labor performed directly for household consumption. In the context of family production relations, where exchange is marginal, any division between labor that is economic (for exchange) and labor that is not is arbitrary. In other words, there is no social mechanism by which it can enter the consciousness of people that part of the activity of living and working must conform to an external norm, while another part need not. Basically, the exchanging family unit in this hypothetical case is involved not in commodity production, but in the production of use values, some of which are exchanged. However wily and avaricious the individual producers may be, they are constrained by their social relations of production in their ability to rationalize their production, because they have no monetary costs. Without monetary costs, there is no vehicle to provide the information to adjust production along economic lines. Certainly all producers, in all circumstances, seek to economize on time, to expend less effort rather than more, but this applies to the entire process of family reproduction, not specifically to production for exchange. Marx makes this point in the *Grundrisse*, when he writes of precapitalist exchange,

> Economy of time, to this all economy ultimately reduces itself. Society likewise has to distribute its time in a purposeful way, in order to achieve a production adequate to its overall needs. . . . Thus, economy of time, along with the planned distribution of labor time among the branches of production, remains the first economic

law on the basis of communal production. . . . However, *this is essentially different from a measurement of exchange values (labor or products) by labor time.* The labor of individuals in *the same branch of work*, and the various kinds of work, are different from one another *not only quantitatively but also qualitatively*.[8]

A distinction can be drawn between the law of the economy of concrete labor time, applicable in all societies with or without exchange, and the law of the minimization of abstract labor time (law of value). The general conclusion that the exchange of products does not in and of itself impose a social standard in production applies even in a case where the family production unit specializes and produces a product that is exchanged in its entirety. As long as inputs are merely use values and not commodities, no mechanism exists to impose an objective standard. The argument that exchanging a product implies a normalization in production is an argument of bourgeois neoclassical theory, the theory of "opportunity cost." There it is argued that individuals survey the opportunities before them, then impute a value to their time based upon the most advantageous alternative. As we shall see, Marx's theory of value turns not upon the perception of individuals, but upon forces external to them, which are reflected in the consciousness of individuals.

To this point we have been considering the case where the producing unit purchases none of the inputs. The role of value as a regulator of exchange is further clarified by considering the next logical stage, where the means of production are monetized. Once a portion of the means of production must be bought, the condition for the repeated cycle of production–exchange changes, since it has now become an extended cycle of exchange-production-exchange. Since money has been advanced prior to production for the means of production, those means of production must be replaced in money form before they can be replaced in material form, a condition not imposed upon the producer in our first hy-

[8] *Ibid.*, p. 173, emphasis added.

pothetical case. The law of exchange takes on a new character, as the price of the production must cover at least the money advanced. As more and more means of production are bought, this imposes as an objective necessity that price cover money costs. Costs now do not reflect the subjective assessment of the producer of his or her expended effort, but an external necessity. The use value emerging from the labor process is becoming a commodity in reality as well as form. In the first case, exchange had an overall indeterminacy quantitatively, since the concrete labor of each producer appeared only as his own labor. In the second case, the means of production are presented to the producer as something separate from him, the product of social labor—the labor of others.[9]

If we consider the historical development of commodity production, as opposed to our hypothetical example, the first major monetization of the means of production comes with the requirement that peasants pay money rent, rather than rent in kind. At this point, it becomes possible to talk of greater determinacy in exchange relations: "The transformation of rent in kind into money-rent, taking place first sporadically and then on a more or less national scale, presupposes a considerable development of commerce, of urban industry, of commodity-production in general, and thereby money circulation. It furthermore assumes a market-price for products and *that they be sold at prices roughly approximating their values, which need not at all be the case under earlier forms.*"[10]

In this quotation Marx is unambiguously clear in saying that commodities do not exchange at value before the development of money rent, a relatively late development; then

[9] "Although the direct producer still continues to produce at least the greater part of his means of subsistence himself, a certain portion of this product must now be converted into commodities, must be produced as commodities. The character of the entire mode of production is thus more or less changed. It loses its independence, its detachment from social connection. The ratio of cost of production, which now comprises greater or lesser expenditures of money, becomes decisive." *Capital*, III, p. 797.

[10] *Ibid.*, emphasis added.

they do so only as a rough approximation. Our point here is not to establish what Marx concluded, but to understand the development of exchange. As long as money costs are few and quantitatively represent a small part of the mass of the means of production, the producer is under no compulsion to exchange his products. If exchange is quantitatively unfavorable, he can retreat into "natural economy" except for those absolutely essential items that can be obtained only in exchange. But as the means of production increasingly take the form of commodities, the product of the labor process *must* be exchanged. A commodity per se is a product that not only is exchangeable but must be exchanged.[11] As the means of production become monetized, the producer is forced to consider the product's exchangeability prior to production; i.e., he must consider it as a commodity from the outset. "The division of a product into a useful thing and a value *becomes practically important only when exchange* has acquired such an extention that useful articles are produced for the purpose of being exchanged *and their character as values has therefore to be taken into account, beforehand, during production.*"[12]

Products become commodities, not in the isolated act of exchange, but insofar as products in general become commodities, and they are stamped as such in the production process, so their subsequent sale does not make them commodities, but is merely one moment in general commodity circulation. As we shall argue later, the moment of circulation always derives from the moment of production,[13] and this generalization applies to commodities as well. When one observes a fully developed commodity-producing (capitalist) society, it appears that products become commodities merely by being exchanged, but this is an illusion, exchange being

[11] *Capital*, I, p. 105.

[12] *Ibid.*, p. 78.

[13] "[T]he intensity of exchange, its extent and structure, are determined by the development and structure of production. . . . A definite production thus determines a definite consumption, distribution and exchange as well as *definite relations between these different moments.*" *Grundrisse*, p. 99.

merely the final moment of commodity circulation. To treat the exchange of products in precapitalist societies as evidence of commodity production is to presuppose the underlying social relations of the most developed form of exchange; particularly the monetization of the means of production.[14]

In this context, we can see that Engels confuses the role of money in exchange. In Engels's view, as we noted in Chapter I, value is a phenomenon of direct perception by individuals, and the general use of money makes this perception more problematical. In reality, the reverse is the case. What one perceives is concrete labor, the actual activity of producing. The transformation of this concrete labor into abstract (value-producing) labor and socially necessary labor is not directly observable. Perception plays no role in the determination of exchange rates, so its role cannot be obscured by money. Rather, the introduction of money forces the producer to consider his costs as a socially imposed norm, which he must recover in exchange or be unable to repeat his production, whatever his perceptions.

At this point it should become clear that under conditions of petty commodity production (self-proprietorship), even if all the means of production are monetized (exchanged for), commodities will not, except as an exception, exchange at their values. This is because a portion of the labor time embodied in commodities so produced remains concrete labor. The living labor expended in production is that of the proprietor and family and is not monetized, and, therefore, not normalized by exchange. This labor remains private; although its product is exchanged against other products, it does not directly enter exchange and become social labor. The rest of the labor embodied in the product must be replaced by money since it has been directly exchanged, but there is no necessity that the living labor be replaced by

[14] And this leads to placing major importance on exchange in precapitalist societies, since the conditions for its full development have been implicitly assumed. Commenting on this, Marx writes, "[I]t is simply wrong to place exchange at the center of a communal society as the original, constituent element." *Ibid.*, p. 103.

money in its entirety, since it never assumed money form before production. Were we dealing with wage labor—capitalist relations of production—then the paid portion of living labor would have to be converted into money and the unpaid portion (surplus value) into profit. Failure to sell the commodity at a price covering wages advanced (plus the money advanced for the means of production, of course) would leave the capitalist unable to re-initiate production at the same level. Failure to realize unpaid labor as profit would mean that the capitalist would lack the money for accumulation. The family-labor production unit does not face these necessities, since accumulation is not relevant—the size of the family sets the limit to the size of the production unit. Marx summarizes this difference well: "For the peasant owning a parcel, the limit of exploitation [lower limit] is not set by the average profit of capital, in so far as he is a small capitalist; nor, on the other hand, by the necessity of rent, in so far as he is a landlord. The absolute limit for him as a small capitalist is no more than the wages he pays to himself, after deducting costs. So long as the price of the product covers these wages, he will cultivate his land and *often at wages down to a physical minimum.*"[15]

This, of course, implies that exchange is not ruled by value, even if the peasant exchanges in a society that is predominantly capitalist. "For the peasant parcel holder to cultivate his land, or to buy land for cultivation, it is therefore not necessary, as under the normal capitalist mode of production, that the market-price of the agricultural products rise high enough to afford him the average profit, and still less a fixed excess above this average profit in the form of rent. *It is not necessary, therefore, that the market-price rise, either up to the value or the price of production of his product.*"[16]

Because living labor is not monetized, "the regulating market-price of the product will reach its value *only under extraordinary circumstances.*"[17] The peasant with unusually

---

[15] *Capital,* III, pp. 805-806. Emphasis added.
[16] *Ibid.,* p. 806. Emphasis added.
[17] *Ibid.,* p. 805.

good land will have expended less working time in producing a given amount of corn, for example, than a less fortunately endowed peasant. As a consequence, the labor of the first peasant is worth more in exchange.[18] The fact that a significant portion of the labor necessary to produce corn is not monetized in this case means there is an indeterminacy in the regulation of price. Value can only act as a regulator of price once the entire product, all inputs, are monetized; until this occurs, the product is not a commodity in its entirety and all the concrete labor time expended on it need not be replaced by money. This, in turn, occurs only with the development of capitalist production.[19]

It is important not to get caught up in a semantical argument. As value has been defined here, it regulates price only under capitalist relations and can be used as a tool of analysis only in capitalist society. Obviously, value reaches its full development as a historical process. Fine, whose analysis of value and the law of value is essentially in agreement with the argument of this chapter, refers to "lower forms of value" which exist in precapitalist society.[20] Certainly, this is a legitimate use of terms, though it has the danger of opening the door to confusion and misinterpretation. The essential point to be made, whatever terms are used, is that only under capitalism is concrete labor in general metamorphosed into abstract labor, and only under capitalism is this necessary in order to bring about the reproduction of class relations.

[18] "One portion of the surplus labor of the peasants, who work under the least favorable conditions, is bestowed gratis upon society and does not at all enter into the regulation of price of production or into the creation of value in general." *Ibid.*, p. 806.

[19] "[T]he product wholly assumes the form of a commodity only—as a result of the fact that the entire product has to be transformed into exchange value and that also all the ingredients necessary for its product enter it as commodities—*in other words it wholly becomes a commodity only with the development and on the basis of capitalist production.*" Karl Marx, *Theories of Surplus Value* (Moscow: Progress Publishers, 1971), III, p. 74. Emphasis added.

[20] Ben Fine, "On Marx's Theory of Agricultural Rent," *Economy and Society* 8, 3 (August 1979).

C. Subjective and Objective Theory of Value

The argument so far can be summarized briefly: the value of a commodity is determined objectively, independently of the perception or knowledge of the exchanging parties, and this objectification of labor time is achieved through the money form. Individuals' judgments as to what portion of their own laboring time or the laboring time of others is necessary for production is merely that—a subjective judgment.[21]

With this in mind, we can roughly categorize the laws of exchange under different modes of production. In all societies, exchange is a part of the general process of social reproduction and governed by the necessity that the society must be reproduced in material and class terms. When exchange is marginal, the production and distribution of use values is, by definition, carried out primarily without exchange. In this case, where few inputs are monetized, exchange is regulated by the condition that the exchange of use values cannot be on terms so unfavorable to the exchanging parties that it leaves those on one side of the exchange unable to satisfy their subsistence needs. If this requirement is not met, one side must cease exchanging and retreat into isolation from market relations. Such a very general law of exchange allows for considerable indeterminacy in exchange ratios, and indeterminacy resolved in practice by the relative power of the exchanging parties. While not wishing to coin a phrase, we might say that, when exchange is infrequent and the means of production unmonetized, it is ruled, for direct producers, by the "law of subsistence."

Once the means of production start to take on a money form, the indeterminacy is reduced, but remains. Here, ex-

[21] Commenting on the work of Bailey, Marx writes: "Their 'mind' [of buyers and sellers], their consciousness, may be completely ignorant of, unaware of the existence of, what in fact determines the value of their products or their products as values. They [buyers and sellers] are placed in relationships which determine their thinking, but they may not know it. . . . Economic categories are reflected in the mind in a very distorted fashion. He [Bailey] transfers the problem into the sphere of consciousness, because his theory has got struck." *Ibid.*, p. 163.

change is ruled by the "law of monetary costs and subsistence." As long as labor power is not monetized, it is not possible to speak of value, except as an externally, idealistically imposed benchmark; it would be an anachronism to do so.[22] When labor power becomes a commodity, under capitalist relations of production, it first becomes possible to apply the concept of value, and the indeterminacy of exchange disappears. At this point, exchange is ruled by the law of value, a law that has two clauses: competition forces all producers to produce with the minimum input of concrete labor time, and forces a tendency toward a normal rate of profit in all industries. These two aspects of the law of value can be called the "law of socially necessary labor time" and the "law of the tendency of the rate of profit to equalize." The law of value involves both, and neither is relevant before capital establishes its dominance over the sphere of production.

Both of these aspects of the law of value are realized through competition; not in Meek's world of "reasonably" competitive independent producers, but through the competition among capitals. The monetization of all inputs coincides with their becoming part of the circuit of capital.[23] generating the first aspect of the law. The movement of capital between branches of industry, predicated upon the availability of free wage labor, tends to equalize the rate of profit across branches. Thus, the law of value, the law of the exchange of equivalent quantities of social labor, is, in fact, the law of surplus value—the law of the appropriation of unpaid labor.[24]

---

[22] Marx criticizes Smith and Ricardo for such anachronistic arguments: "Although Adam Smith determines the value of commodities by the labor-time contained in them, he then nevertheless transfers this determination of value in actual fact to pre-Smithian times. . . . [Ricardo] slips into the anachronism of allowing the primitive fisherman and hunter to calculate the value of implements." Marx, A Contribution, p. 60.

[23] The means of production exchange against constant capital and labor power against variable capital.

[24] Colletti states this well, "In conclusion: the law of value which is indeed a law of exchange of *equivalents*, as soon as it is realized and becomes *domi-*

D. The "Necessary Illusion"

The task of theory is not only to explain reality but, through that explanation, to account for why other theories would explain the same reality differently. To this point, we have engaged only in the former task: to develop the concept of value and demonstrate the circumstances under which it becomes socially significant as a regulator of the interactions of producers. The question remains as to why anyone (and particularly Marx's life-long collaborator, Engels) would view value in a completely different and opposed way. This is not a mere exercise in the history of economic thought, but a task that allows one to reveal starkly the illusions—obfuscating forms—generated by the process of the circulation of capital. In other words, the labor theory of value is not only a theory of the social regulation of production but a theory of how that production becomes *fetishized*—why it appears as something it is not.[25]

Engels begins with commodity exchange on the basis of equivalent exchange (commodities exchanging at their values) in a context in which each producer has the right to his labor. Marx begins similarly, with no explicit statement as to the social relations of production involved. But from this starting point, the two distinct approaches emerge and the theoretical arguments go separate ways. In the former case, the presumption that individuals hold right to their labor is never questioned, but maintained throughout, and social relations of production are not considered at all, until it becomes necessary to deal with the historical reality of capitalism. In the latter case, the analysis reveals, step by step, that the assumption of individual private property is inconsistent with the actual operation of the law of value and must be

nant, reveals its true nature as the law of *surplus value* and capitalist appropriation." Lucio Colletti, *From Rousseau to Lenin* (New York: Monthly Review Press, 1979), p. 95.

[25] "Marx's theory of value is identical to his *theory of fetishism* and it is precisely by virtue of this element . . . that Marx's theory differs in principle from the whole of classical political economy." Colletti, *ibid.*, p. 77.

discarded.[26] For Marx, the right to one's labor was *merely an assumption*; for Engels it characterized an actual society.

In bourgeois society, wealth presents itself as commodities, and, if we abstract from the circulation of capital, commodity circulation appears as the exchange of equivalents. If we ignore the social relations under which commodities are produced and begin with a particular commodity already in the market, what we observe is the commodity exchanged by the seller for money; then the seller uses the money to buy another commodity. Marx called this sequence "simple commodity circulation" and symbolized it in the notation C-M-C. Viewed in isolation, C-M-C implies by definition no exploitation. But as we have seen in previous sections, this assumption of equal exchange presupposes a quantitative measure of "equalness." This quantitative measure is value, or rather, the magnitude of value. This measure, in turn, presupposes that the means of production and labor power are commodities, i.e., capitalist relations of production. In the absence of these social relations, the equivalence is merely formal, in that it is not based on socially necessary labor time. Only under capitalist relations is it possible to compare the living labor objectified in commodities and make the formal equivalence an equivalence in essence. Thus, we can begin by assuming individual property in commodities, but will quickly discover that our starting point, the simple circulation of commodities, implies the circulation of capital. We discover that C-M-C (commodities-money-commodities) implies M-C-M', the advance of money as capital for labor power and the means of production (M-C), the exploitation of labor in production, and the subsequent realization of the commodities as money capital. What we have discovered is that C-M-C is not "simple" in the sense of predating capitalism, but subsumed in capital's circulation as the

---

[26] Marx subsequently comments on his assumption made in Chapter I of Volume I, "At first the rights of property seemed to us to be based on a man's own labor. At least, some such *assumption* was necessary since only commodity-owners with equal rights confronted each other." *Capital*, I, p. 547. Emphasis added.

exchange forced upon the proletariat. Workers exchange their commodity, labor power, for money, then use this money to obtain their means of subsistence. To re-initiate the circuit, they must offer their working capacity again for sale. Capitalists, on the other hand, as part of the same exchange advance money for labor power and receive at the end of their circuit an expanded quantity of money. Equal exchange (C-M-C) is merely a derivative part of a social relationship of exploitation.

This logical progression reveals the social reality beneath the exchange of equivalents. Commodity exchange is ruled by value when labor power itself is a commodity, which necessarily implies the historical process by which labor has been separated from the means of production. With this separation, workers must sell their labor power in order to obtain their means of subsistence, and capitalists must buy it in order to initiate production. Thus, the exchange of equivalents is an illusion since it is based upon the buying and selling of labor power, which involves the appropriation of unpaid labor (surplus value). This appropriation occurs in production, as the capitalist consumes the use value of labor power, forcing the worker to labor the full working day, beyond the time necessary to produce the commodities equivalent to the value of labor power.

The illusion of equivalent exchange is not a mere ruse but necessary. Capitalist competition enforces a tendency toward minimization of concrete labor and equalization of the rate of profit across branches of industry. Thus the equivalence involved is an equivalence among capitalists, whereby each tends to receive an equal "reward" for the capital he or she puts in motion.[27] For the worker, the equivalence is of a different sort, since he or she has only labor power to sell. For this class, the sale of labor power at its value is equality in form, but exploitation in essence, since the worker surren-

[27] Here we abstract from the transformation of values into prices of production, which does not affect the argument.

ders the right to the product of his or her labor by virtue of the exchange.[28]

The illusion of equal exchange, or the equal-exchange-appropriation-of-unpaid-labor contradiction, corresponds to the illusion of private property under capitalist relations of production. A world of commodity exchange is formally or legalistically based upon private property, but this is merely formal. As a legal fiction, all persons in a capitalist society are guaranteed the right to private property, the right to hold, accumulate, and alienate wealth. However, in reality, the operation of capitalist society presupposes the negation of this right. Capitalist accumulation is based upon the appropriation of unpaid labor through the buying and selling of labor power. For society as a whole, labor power becomes a commodity when the masses of the population are separated from their means of production—their property is expropriated by the process Marx called "primitive accumulation."[29] Capitalist private property is not a system of individual rights to property, but the monopolization of the means of production by the bourgeoisie.[30]

[28] Marx summarizes this contradiction between appearance and reality as follows: "Production based on exchange value and the community based on the exchange of these exchange values—even though they seem . . . to posit property as the outcome of *labor* alone, and to posit private property over the product of one's own labor as condition—and labor as general condition of wealth, *all presuppose and produce the separation of labor from its objective conditions*. This exchange of equivalents proceeds; it is only the *surface layer* [emphasis added] of a production which rests on the appropriation of alien labor *without exchange*, but with the *semblance of exchange*. This system of exchange rests on *capital* as its foundation, and when it is regarded in isolation from capital, then it is a mere illusion, but a necessary illusion. Thus there is no longer any ground for astonishment that the system of exchange values—*exchange of equivalents through labor*—turns into, or rather *reveals as its hidden background*, complete separation of labor and property [emphasis added]." *Grundrisse*, p. 509.

[29] "The so-called primitive accumulation, therefore, is nothing else than the historical process of divorcing the producer from the means of production." *Capital*, I, p. 668.

[30] "Political Economy confuses on principle two very different kinds of private property, of which one rests on the producer's own labor, the other on the employment of the labor of others. It forgets that the latter not only

The appropriation of unpaid labor—direct and obvious in systems of slavery and serfdom—appears as the exchange of equivalents under capitalism; this facade of equality reflects a facade of private property for all, and conceals the fact that the only property of the worker is his or her capacity to labor. Further, this "property" alienable by the worker can only be sold to capitalists. The law of exchange under capitalism is as follows: capitalists exchange at value and appropriate surplus value and accumulate; workers exchange at value and surrender unpaid labor.[31]

The recognition that the law of value first became operative under capitalism and not before is a scientific insight of considerable political importance and is the cutting edge of Marxism's attack on reformist political practice.[32] To argue that the law of value ruled for five to seven thousand years, as Engels does (and Meek for a more modest period), is to argue that exchange can occur among independent, self-employed producers without generating capitalism. That is, it posits a world of competing producers, exchanging their labor, without any contradictions that would give rise to the concentration and centralization of production. In short, implicit in the argument is that commodity exchange itself can be equal and socially egalitarian, and is characterized by exploitation only when it comes under the domination of capital. This view, commodity production and the competition among producers that it implies, treats exchange as intrinsically benign, capable of regulating and reproducing a society of equals. This, in turn, implies that commodity production and competition are not themselves sources of exploitation,

is the direct antithesis of the former, but absolutely grows on its tomb only." *Ibid.*, p. 716.

[31] "[A]ccording to Marx, what makes this relation of equality *formal* and conceals real inequality is the fact that the property at the disposal of the worker (his own laboring *capacity*) is only property in *appearance*." Colletti, *From Rousseau to Lenin*, p. 94.

[32] Colletti goes so far as to say, "This confusion between law of labor time (which applies to all societies) and its fetishized realization in the world of capital and of commodities [law of value] . . . *is the root of modern revisionism*." *Ibid.*, p. 91. Emphasis added.

economic crisis, etc., but only become so under capitalism. Another way of saying this is that the contradiction between use value and exchange value is not antagonistic. From this it follows that commodity production need not be abolished to end the crises, class antagonisms, etc., associated with capitalism.

This, of course, was precisely the argument of Proudhon, which Marx attacked so sharply.[33] He did so because the production of commodities necessarily implies capitalism, and as it develops it generates capitalists and proletarians. If one does not recognize this, it is possible to believe that regulation of the abuses capitalism generates within commodity production will have a major impact on eliminating the class antagonisms of the system and the tendency toward crises.

The debate over whether commodity exchange itself implies capitalist exploitation has a long history in Marxist literature. It is over exactly this issue that Lenin berated the "Norodnik" economists in Russia. Like Proudhon (and Engels), these spokesmen of the peasantry argued that a society of independent, proprietor farmers and craftsmen could form the basis of a commodity-producing society and that capitalism distorted commodity production. Lenin rejected this romantic view, arguing that independent commodity production necessarily implies capitalism,

> [S]eparate producers, each producing commodities on his own for the market, enter into competition with one another: each strives to sell at the highest price and to buy at the lowest, *a necessary result of which is that the strong become stronger and the weak go under*, a minority are enriched and the masses are ruined. This leads to the conversion of independent producers into wage-workers and of numerous small enterprises into a few big ones.
>
> The enrichment of a few individuals and the impover-

[33] Marx does this in *The Poverty of Philosophy*.

ishment of the masses—such are the inevitable consequences of the law of competition.[34]

Given the conditions for general commodity production—
producers untied to the land or guilds by servile social relations—one has the conditions for the development of capitalism. The spread of commodity circulation necessarily
leads by its own laws of competition to the negation of independent, separate, and isolated producers. Commodity
production appears as the exchange of equivalents, but necessarily implies the division of society into the two great antagonistic classes of modern times—the capitalist class and
the proletariat.

E. The Law of Value Summarized

Having established the historical specificity of the law of
value—that it applies to capitalist relations of production
alone—we can now summarize its operation. In every society a division of labor must be brought about such that the
products produced conform in variety and quantity to the
necessity of social reproduction. In precapitalist society, this
division of labor is achieved through a conscious regulation
prior to production and distribution. This is achieved through
largely servile social relations—slavery and serfdom being
the best known examples. With the separation of labor from
the means of production, production becomes socially isolated, with each capitalist arriving at his or her production
decisions in a formally independent manner. It is in this sense
that capitalist production is anarchic.

This anarchy is both reflected in and rendered into an or-
derly anarchy through exchange. Conceptually, the first consequence of this exchange is that each capitalist is forced to
produce in an efficient way. The exchange of the means of
production and labor power presents each capitalist with a
standardized monetary cost for a given quantity of these.

---

[34] V. I. Lenin, "On the So-Called Market Question," in *Collected Works*
(Moscow: Progress Publishers, 1972), pp. 93, 95.

These quantities must then be consumed productively subject to a standardized selling price. As some capitals consume productive capital more efficiently, their profits increase accordingly, and the less efficient capitals must emulate the more efficient or be eliminated from production. It is by this process that socially necessary labor time is established in each industry. The concrete labor consumed in production—living and dead—is rendered comparable in exchange and normalized through competition. In this manner, value comes to rule production. The socially determined normal labor time exists "behind the backs" of each capitalist, and without entering the consciousness of capitalists regulates their production. This is the operation of the law of the minimization of concrete labor in production.

In the accumulation process, qualitative changes—productivity change, concentration, and centralization—result in a change in the quantitative distribution (composition) of total production. At this point, the law of value becomes the law of the social division of labor. Shifts in supply and demand result in deviations of exchange value from value, resulting in profitability deviating systematically across branches of industry. This deviation, which manifests itself in profit differentials, is reduced by the movement of capital between industries. In this process by which workers are shifted between industries, concrete labor, rendered abstract through the exchange of the products of their labor, becomes abstract directly. The shift of labor between branches of industry by capital separates in practice particular concrete labor carried out in the labor process from the worker himself or herself. There increasingly comes to be no relationship between the particular knowledge or skill of the worker and the work he or she carries out. With the mobility of the proletariat among labor processes, the worker's labor power is rendered an abstract force, alien to him.[35]

The law of value, then, is not only the law of labor time under capitalism (division of labor), the law of surplus value

---

[35] *Capital*, I, pp. 402ff.

(exploitation), but also the mechanism of alienation. When capitalism is immature and laborers carry to the capitalist-controlled labor process skills and knowledge necessary for production, this alienation is primarily the alienation of the worker from his product. As capitalism develops and the division of labor increases within the production process, the worker increasingly becomes alienated from the work process itself, reduced to a mere source of homogeneous, abstract human energy. The worker becomes in form and essence merely an extension of capital, so that the cooperative productive power of the masses appears as the productive power of capital.[36]

[36] *Capital*, I, Chap. XIII.

APPENDIX

THE VIEWS OF MARX AND ENGELS
ON THE LAW OF VALUE

A. INTRODUCTION

Friedrich Engels is a towering figure in the history of the revolutionary movement. It is a serious matter for one to take basic exception to his views, particularly since there is an unfortunate tendency in the Marxist literature to rely upon quotations from authorities rather than scientific argument. In Chapter II, we used quotations—particularly from Marx—only when their clarity was so striking that they cried out for inclusion. Our purpose in this appendix is to reach into the work of Marx and Engels to demonstrate unambiguously that their views on fundamental issues differed diametrically. The issues considered here are: (1) the historical specificity of the law of value, (2) the role of perception and knowledge in the operation of that law, and (3) the process of the transition from precapitalist modes of production to the capitalist mode of production.

B. THE HISTORICAL SPECIFICITY OF THE LAW OF VALUE

In Chapter I, we demonstrated that Engels believed that the law of value had operated for five to seven thousand years, and it is not necessary to quote from his work again to that effect. It remains only to establish Marx's criticism of such an interpretation.

By drawing together Marx's different works, it is possible to present a coherent critique of Engels's analysis of exchange. As we saw in Chapter I, Engels begins his treatment of exchange by considering a society of independent producers, producing a surplus, in which this surplus is exchanged individually to satisfy needs that each producer cannot satisfy by his own production. We have here the presupposition of individual property in the product of labor, the existence of a surplus, and a complex division of labor. Marx rejected each of these presuppositions explicitly. Writing of the pre-capitalist period, he says,

> [Merchant's capital] therefore merely promotes the exchange of commodities, yet this exchange *is not to be conceived* at the outset as a bare exchange of commodities *between direct producers*. Under slavery, feudalism, vassalage . . . it is the *slave-owner, the feudal lord, the tribute-collecting state, who are the owners, hence sellers, of the products*.[1] [Emphasis added.]

This exchange is among members of the exploiting classes, because property, in Marx's view, was not held privately, but was essentially communal, and the individual was only an organic part of the community.

> The earth is the great workshop, the arsenal which furnishes both means and material of labor, as well as the seat, the *base* of the community, of the community producing and reproducing itself in living labor. Each individual conducts himself only as a link, as a member of this community as *proprietor* or *possessor*.[2]

This, according to Marx, implied that the individual cannot be considered as a worker.[3] Further, the existence of a surplus product is not a natural thing, but must be explained in terms of the social relations that create it; "favorable natural conditions alone, give us *only the possibility*, never the reality, of surplus labor."[4] The presupposition of private property and a surplus product is necessary for Engels's

[1] *Capital*, III, p. 326.
[2] *Grundrisse*, p. 472.
[3] *Ibid.*, pp. 471-472.
[4] *Theories of Surplus Value*, p. 460 and *Capital*, I, pp. 482-483. Engels's presupposition of a surplus product is also made by Meek, but more explicitly: "I assume that [a surplus product] is in fact produced, but that at first it is consumed by the direct producers." Meek, *Smith, Marx and After* (London: Chapman and Hall, 1977), p. 133.

treatment of the division of labor. As we saw in Chapter I, Engels believed that the division of labor arose spontaneously and naturally because "[the peasant] lacked the raw material or because the purchased article was much better or very much cheaper."[5] This formulation assumes what it seeks to establish; i.e., it assumes that families "had to obtain" some things they required, which presupposes the need for things, and presupposes that specialization exists. Here Engels is following in the logic of Proudhon,[6] which Marx attacked sharply,

> A very large number of products are not to be found in nature [Proudhon says]. . . . If man's needs go beyond nature's spontaneous production, he is forced to have recourse to individual production. . . . A single individual, feeling the need for a very great number of things, 'cannot set his hand to so many things' [i.e., make them 'very much cheaper,' JW]. [However] so many needs to satisfy *presuppose so many to produce*—there are no products without production. . . . Now, *the moment you postulate more than one man's hand helping in production, you at once presuppose a whole production based on the division of labor*. Thus need . . . itself presupposes the whole division of labor. In presupposing the division of labor, you get exchange, and, consequently, exchange value. One might as well have presupposed exchange value from the very beginning.[7]

Thus, by postulating that some can produce things cheaper and better, Engels presupposes the need for them in the first place and the division of labor that allows for some to pro-

---

[5] *Capital*, III, p. 897.

[6] "How does use value become exchange value? . . . Since a very large number of things I need occur in nature only in moderate quantities, or even not at all, I am forced to assist in the production of what I lack. And as I cannot set my hand to many things, I shall *propose* to other men . . . to cede to me a part of their products in *exchange* for mine." Proudhon, *Philosophy of Poverty*, quoted in Marx and Engels, *Collected Works*, VI, p. 111.

[7] *Ibid.*, pp. 111-112.

duce them cheaper and better. This, of course, implies that exchange arises voluntarily and individualistically. Having assumed the division of labor, assumed many needs, and assumed, in effect, exchange, Engels then considers the quantitative basis of exchange. For him, this derives from the answer to a rhetorical question,

> What had [the producers] expended in making these products? Labor and labor alone. . . . [T]hey spent nothing but their own labor power.[8]

It is exactly such a statement which Marx criticized in the Gotha Program ("Labor is the source of wealth"). While it is true by definition that human beings expend only their labor power on a product, this implies nothing in and of itself until one specifies the social relations within which that labor power is carried out,

> Labor is *not the source* of all wealth. Nature is just as much the source of use value . . . as labor. . . . Man's labor only becomes a source of use values, and hence also of wealth, if his relation to nature, the primary source of all instruments and objects of labor, is one of ownership from the start.[9]

Thus the answer to Engels's question presupposes private ownership, which he assumes *ex machina*. Totally ignored are the social relations of production of peasant society and the exploitation that was the basis of that class society. Marx's entire treatment of exchange in precapitalist society is based upon the recognition that these societies were characterized by servile relations of production in which the direct producers, while united with the means of production, had no right of property. Because they did not and the closely related reason that the means of production were not monetized, value did not rule exchange. Criticizing Torrens, Marx makes this explicit,

[8] *Capital*, III, p. 897.
[9] Karl Marx, *The First International and After* (New York: Vintage Books, 1974), p. 341.

"In that early period of society" [Torrens's phrase] (that is, precisely when exchange value in general, the product as a commodity, is hardly developed at all, and consequently *when there is no law of value either*).[10]

The law of value does not exist because,

[T]he product wholly assumes the form of a commodity only as a result of the fact that the entire product has to be transformed into exchange value and that also all the ingredients necessary for its production enter it as commodities—in other words it wholly becomes a commodity only with the development and on the basis of capitalist production.[11]

Marx again and again repeats that value rules *only* under capitalism, that the exchange of equivalents that Engels places in precapitalist times occurs only under capitalism and hides exploitation. In Chapter II (footnote 28) we gave a quotation from the *Grundrisse* to this effect. Almost the same passage appears in *Capital*, Volume I,

[I]t is evident that the laws of appropriation or of private property, laws that are based on the production and circulation of commodities, become by their own inner and inexorable dialectic changed into their very opposite. The exchange of equivalents, *the original operation with which we started*, has now become turned round in such a way that there is *only an apparent exchange*.[12]

This inversion does not occur historically, but is the relationship between surface appearance ("necessary illusion") and the underlying reality,

At first, the rights of property seemed to us to be based on a man's own labor. At least, some such *assumption* was necessary since only commodity-owners with equal rights confronted each other, and the sole means by

[10] *Theories of Surplus Value*, III, p. 73.
[11] *Ibid*.
[12] *Capital*, I, p. 547.

which a man could become possessed of the commodities of others, was by alienating his own commodities. . . . Now, however, property turns out to be the right, on the part of the capitalist, to appropriate the unpaid labor of others or its product, and to be the impossibility, on the part of the laborer, of appropriating his own product. The separation of property from labor has become the necessary consequence of a law that *apparently* originated in their identity. [Emphasis added.]¹³

Having made this line of argument, Marx refers sarcastically to a society of independent producers exchanging equivalents as the "paradise lost of the bourgeoisie, where people did not confront one another as capitalists, wage-earners, landowners, tenant farmers, usurers, and so on, but simply as persons who produced commodities and sold them."¹⁴ It is exactly such a lost paradise of unexploited producers that Engels creates in order to analyze exchange.

B. The Role of Perception
and Knowledge of Labor Time

As we have seen, Engels explained equivalent exchange on the basis of the knowledge of producers—having knowledge of the production of others, the exchanging parties would be "stupid" to accept other than equivalent exchange. In Chapter II, we showed that this explanation confuses concrete and abstract labor, and we need not repeat that argument (or Marx's views given there). For Marx, the law of value was an objective law, independent of perception,

> The "circumstances" which determine the value of a commodity are by no means further elucidated by being described as circumstances which influence the "mind" of those engaging in exchange, as circumstances which, as such, likewise exist (or perhaps they do not, or per-

¹³ *Ibid.*
¹⁴ *A Contribution*, p. 60.

haps they are incorrectly conceived) in the consciousness of those engaging in exchange.[15]

In his movement from labor-in-production to price, Engels is again following the method of Proudhon, which Marx ridiculed,

> Begin, he [Proudhon] says, by measuring the relative value of a product by the quantity of labor embodied in it, and supply and demand will infallibly balance one another. . . . [T]he product's price will express exactly its true value.[16]

This is Engels's argument: each buyer measures labor time in production by observation, then exchange reflects this assessment. Marx comments:

> Instead of saying like everyone else: when the weather is fine, a lot of people are to be seen going out for a walk, M. Proudhon makes his people go out for a walk in order to be able to ensure them fine weather.[17]

Marx's analogy makes the point that value only appears as price, and it is only in the form—the price form—which values affect the consciousness of the parties involved in the exchange. The essence of the value-price relationship for Engels is that the two are identical: individual knowledge of values, prior to exchange, brings about exchange at value. Thus, like Proudhon, for Engels "people go for a walk in order to be able to ensure them fine weather." For Marx, the essence of the value-price relationship is their non-equivalence.

> But although price . . . is the exponent of [a commodity's] exchange ratio with money, it does not follow that the exponent of this exchange value is necessarily the exponent of the magnitude of the commodity's value.[18]

---

[15] *Theories of Surplus Value*, III, p. 163.
[16] Marx and Engels, *Collected Works*, VI, p. 131.
[17] *Ibid.*
[18] *Capital*, I, p. 104.

The deviation of price from value signals commodity producers to vary their supply by momentarily allowing producers to realize above or below normal profits. Thus the law of value is not the result of knowledge, but "competition implements the law according to which the relative value of a product is determined by the labor time needed to produce it," and, further, this implies that "the determination of value by labor time . . . is therefore merely the scientific expression *of the economic relations of present-day society.*" [Emphasis added.][19]

In summary, Engels's stress on perception arises from not considering the social relations within which exchange occurs. Having abstracted from social relations, he necessarily treats exchange ahistorically and makes value an abstraction of the mind in the first instance. Marx argued the opposite— the minds of people form abstractions only when those abstractions exist in reality, independently of whether they are perceived.[20]

C. The Transition to Capitalism

Engels argued that the development of capitalism could be explained in "purely economic" terms, "without the necessity for recourse in a single instance" to any "political inference."[21] Marx devoted an entire section of Volume I of *Capital* to the forceable methods that accompanied the emergence of capitalism. Indeed, the titles of the chapters in this section indicate his view of the role of violence. Chapters XXVI-XXXIII of Volume I represent almost a continuous analysis of the violence necessary for the emergence of the capitalist mode of production.[22]

One quotation suffices to demonstrate Marx's view:

[19] Marx and Engels, *Collected Works*, VI, p. 134.

[20] *Grundrisse*, p. 106.

[21] *Anti-Duhring*, p. 208.

[22] It is noteworthy that in his reviews and summary of Volume I of *Capital*, Engels does not refer to these chapters. Friedrich Engels, *On Marx's Capital* (Moscow: Progress Publishers, 1972).

Direct force, outside of economic conditions, is of course still used, but only exceptionally [in nineteenth century Britain]. . . . *It is otherwise during the historical genesis of capitalist production.* The bourgeoisie, at its rise, wants and uses the power of the state to "regulate" wages, i.e., to force them within the limits suitable for surplus value making, to lengthen the working day and to keep the laborer himself in the normal degree of dependence. *This is an essential element of the so-called primitive accumulation.*[23]

This is a particular case of Marx's general conclusion that "force is the midwife of every old society pregnant with a new one."[24]

The other elements of Engels's view of the transition—that it was brought about by merchant's capital, that it involved artisans voluntarily choosing wage labor—were also criticized by Marx when he found these arguments in the work of others. On the latter question, Marx argued that the apparently voluntary acceptance of wage slavery occurred only because workers had forceably been separated from their means of production and had no choice but to become proletarians. He viewed self-employment as a barrier to the development of capitalism, which had to be eliminated through the force of the state.[25]

Equally important from a theoretical point of view is Engels's incorrect treatment of merchant's capital. In Marx's view, merchant's capital was the form of capital (M-C-M') without the essence of capital (control over production). As a consequence:

[All] development of merchant's capital tends to give production more and more the character of production for exchange value and to turn products more and more into commodities. *Yet its development . . . is incapable by*

[23] Emphasis added. *Capital*, I, p. 689.
[24] *Ibid.*, p. 703.
[25] See *Grundrisse*, pp. 505-508; *Capital*, I, pp. 681-685, 686, 694.

itself of promoting and explaining the transition from one mode of production to another.[26]

Marx does consider the case of the merchant extending his control over production and comes to a conclusion opposite to that of Engels,

This system presents everywhere an obstacle to the real capitalist mode of production and goes under with its development.[27]

In Marx's view, capitalism develops by virtue of the direct producer becoming a capitalist:

The transition from the feudal mode of production is twofold. The producer becomes merchant and capitalist. . . . This is the really revolutionizing path. Or else, the merchant establishes direct sway over production. However much this serves historically as a stepping stone . . . it cannot by itself contribute to the overthrow of the old mode of production, but tends rather to preserve and retain it as its precondition.[28]

Thus, for Marx, merchant's capital did not provide the path to capitalism, since it was incapable of generating the separation of labor from the means of production ("primitive accumulation").

As a final note, it should be pointed out that Marx and Engels had entirely different explanations of the origin of surplus value in the initial stages of capitalist development. Engels, as part of his voluntaristic view of the development of wage labor, argued that independent artisans willingly accepted lower wages in exchange for regular employment. The idea that capitalists (and capitalism) can deliver "regular employment" is in-and-of-itself a quite astounding idea, when one realizes that the capitalist mode of production is

[26] *Capital*, III, p. 327. Emphasis added.
[27] *Ibid.*, p. 334.
[28] *Ibid.*, p. 334.

the first to generate idleness for a part of the laboring population as an endemic and *systematic* characteristic of its operation. Indeed, even if we only consider employment at the level of individual capitals, a basic advantage of capitalist relations of production is precisely that capitalists can hire and fire workers at will. This is a necessary characteristic for a mode of production based on production for exchange value and constant revolutionizing of the means of production. Inherent in capitalist accumulation is what Marx called "that monstrosity, an industrial reserve army, kept in misery in order to be always at the disposal of capital," and the reserve army and the fluctuations of the market "dispels all fixity and security in the situation of the laborer."[29] Engels clearly reverses reality. It is the control of the means of production that gives the direct producer any security at all, and separation from the means of production eliminates that security.

Only slightly less astonishing is the argument that producers would willingly accept a lower standard of living, even if such security of employment were magically guaranteed. Such an explanation for the production of surplus value comes very close to the arguments of a social contract type.[30]

Marx's explanation of surplus value was entirely different. First, the forced, violent process of the separation of labor from the means of production (particularly land) created a free, impoverished proletariat which had the "choice" of vagabondage or wage-slavery. Given a large pool of free-wage labor, impoverished and politically powerless, capitalists could force down the standard of living of their workers to a base minimum and ruthlessly extend the working day.[31]

[29] *Capital*, I, p. 457.

[30] "How then, in old Europe, was the expropriation of the laborer from his conditions of labor, i.e., the coexistence of capital and labor, brought about? By a social contract of a quite original kind [according to E. G. Wakefield]. 'Mankind have adopted a . . . simple contrivance for promoting the accumulation of capital,' which, of course, since the time of Adam, floated in their imagination . . . : 'they have divided themselves into owners of capital and owners of labor. This division was the result of concert and combination.' " *Ibid.*, p. 718. Marx is quoting from Wakefield here.

[31] See *Capital*, I, Chapter XI and also X ("The Working Day").

D. Origin of the Opposing Views

We have shown the fundamental disagreements between Marx and Engels over the analysis of capitalism. It is possible, in very general terms, to identify the origins of the differences. In *The German Ideology*, written by Marx and Engels in the 1840s, one finds a theoretical method that places circulation and production on the same analytical level, codetermining the development of society.[32] Engels never changed from this position:

> Political economy, in the widest sense, is the science of the laws governing the production and exchange of the material means of subsistence in human society. . . . [E]ach has what are also for a large part *its own special laws*. But on the other hand, they constantly determine and influence each other to such an extent that they might be termed the abscissa and ordinate of the economic curve.[33]

Certainly by the time he came to write *A Contribution to the Critique of Political Economy*, Marx had totally broken with this position. In the *Grundrisse* he makes this clear, dealing first with distribution[34] then exchange in regard to production:

> But (1) no exchange is possible without division of labor, whether this is naturally evolved or is already the result of a historical process; (2) private exchange presupposes private production; (3) *the intensity of exchange, its extent and nature, are determined by the development and structure of production.*

[32] Karl Marx and Friedrich Engels, *The German Ideology* (New York: International Publishers, 1972), p. 58.

[33] *Anti-Duhring*, p. 186.

[34] Marx writes, "the structure of distribution is completely determined by the structure of production" [*Grundrisse*, p. 95]. Compare to Engels, "Distribution, however, is not a merely passive result of production and exchange; *it reacts just as much on both.*" *Anti-Duhring*, p. 190, emphasis added.

Production is the decisive phase both with regard to the contradictory aspects of production *and with regard to the other phases.* [Emphasis added.][35]

In general terms, the theoretical differences between Marx and Engels derive from the fact that Engels remained a circulationist throughout his writings and, for all his contributions, never grasped the "real science of modern economy,"

The science of modern economy only begins when the theoretical analysis passes from the process of circulation to the process of production.[36]

[35] *Grundrisse*, p. 139. See also, *A Contribution*, p. 204, where the same phrase is found.
[36] *Capital*, III, p. 337.

CHAPTER III

EXPLOITATION AND THE RATE
OF SURPLUS VALUE

A. Social Production and
the Rate of Surplus Value

In the previous chapters we have developed the explanation of the law of value that locates value at the social rather than the individual level. We can reformulate our critique of the "embodied labor time" view of value in this way. The argument of Engels and of those who move directly from concrete labor to exchange value is that value (embodied labor time) not only arises in production but is directly translated into exchange value without the interaction of producers as commodity sellers. Following Marx, we have argued that value originates in production, in that the expenditure of living labor is the only source of value, but the particular concrete labor time expended in each work process does not measure the magnitude of value; first, because it is concrete, not abstract labor, and, second, because it may be above or below the normal labor time imposed by the interaction of capitals (competition). Value is socially necessary abstract labor time, and each producer's value creation is but a fractional ("aliquot") part of total social labor. In each work process, concrete labor is expended, then rendered abstract in exchange; the interaction of capitals generates a social norm that each capital must emulate, and the abstract labor created under the domination of each capital appears as part of society's total socialized labor.[1]

---

[1] "[T]here is no way to reduce observable concrete labor to social abstract labor in advance, outside of the market which actually effects the reduction." Gerstein, "Production, Circulation and Value," *Economy and Society* (August 1976), p. 8. All in italics in original.

Just as value has a real existence separate from each particular production process, so exploitation is a social (society-wide) phenomenon under capitalism. While the exploitation of labor by capital occurs in production, through the capitalist's consumption of the use value of labor power, the total mass of surplus value and the rate of surplus value are determined in abstraction from each labor process. Thus the quantity and rate of surplus value are in the first instance social or society-wide, not the result of an aggregation of quantities and rates prevailing in each workplace.

This characteristic of exploitation, which reflects the socialized nature of production under capitalism, is clarified by considering exploitation in precapitalist society, particularly peasant-feudal society. In what broadly can be called "feudal society," production was economically isolated, but directly social within production units. It was economically isolated in that each manor—the area over which the landlord's authority extended—was largely self-contained. Inputs—the means of production—were not exchanged between production units to any great degree. To the extent that the domains of landlords were linked, this linkage was purely in the social relations between landlords and higher authorities. The linkages reflected the social organization of society, not the links of an intermingled production matrix.

As a consequence, differences in the productivity of labor between production units, even between peasant holdings within these units, was particular to each unit. The level of production (of use values) depended upon differences in fertility of the soil, the particularities of the landholding pattern, and other characteristics internal to the manor. Similarly, the size of the surplus product appropriated by the exploiting class depended upon these characteristics and the degree of oppression the exploiting class could bring to bear upon the direct producers. In any social system there is a tendency toward normalization of social practice, for reasons of custom if no other. But since land was not alienable nor peasants freely mobile to any significant degree, there was no mechanism, short of a local revolt of peasants, to bring about a normalization of productive efficiency and degree of exploitation.[2] Under capitalism, by contrast, the movement of capital would tend to eliminate the relatively unfertile land from production. When land cannot be bought and sold, the landed exploiter has no choice but to use the land over which he had been granted rights.

In such a society, the distinction between necessary labor and surplus labor was direct and obvious. The work of the peasant was clearly divided between the time he worked for his family and the time he worked for the landlord. This division often took the form of the peasant laboring a certain number of days per year in the landlord's fields, in which case the actual work itself was divided. Alternatively, or in combination with this, the peasant delivered a portion of his production directly to the landlord. In this context it is possible to distinguish objectively between necessary labor, the labor necessary to reproduce the peasant family, and surplus labor, the labor performed for the exploiter of labor, since this division existed in reality.[3] However, it is not possible to speak of a rate of exploitation for society as a whole.

A rate of exploitation requires that the concrete labor of the direct producer be reducible to abstract labor in order to be aggregated; and in the absence of exchange, no such reduction occurs in reality, so to do it conceptually is purely arbitrary. Products are not rendered commensurate in fact, and it would be arbitrary to impose this upon them.

It is, however, heuristically useful to create a hypothetical feudal society in which a measurement of exploitation is formally possible. Let us assume we have a society of largely self-sufficient feudal manors in which only one product is produced—corn. Assume further that the standard of living (necessary corn) is the same for all peasants. In this hypothetical society, there is a "rate of exploitation" for the society as a whole (the ratio of surplus corn to necessary corn), but this aggregate rate has no social significance; it exists

[2] Robert Brenner, "The Origins of Capitalist Development," *New Left Review*, 104 (July–August 1977).
[3] See *Capital*, I, p. 227.

only as a numerical average of each individual rate of exploitation. Each isolated rate of exploitation in this case is the result of the particularities of the soil and social organization internal to the unit of social production. Since the means of production and labor power are not commodities, there is no tendency for individual rates of exploitation to move toward the societal average. In our hypothetical society, and precapitalist society in general, labor was directly social in that it was characterized by conscious organization directly between people, but production was not socialized, by which we mean integrated for society as a whole.

Capitalism involves precisely the opposite: labor expended in production is not directly social, but production necessarily becomes socialized. With the separation of the direct producer from the means of production and the division of labor that implies, self-sufficient production comes to an end, and each producer's productive activity becomes dependent objectively upon the activity of other producers. Thus we have the contradiction that there are no direct social links between producers, but these producers are necessarily enmeshed in an interdependent production system. As we have seen, it is value that resolves this contradiction by establishing norms in the use and allocation of concrete labor that are independent of each producer (each capital).

We can now locate the rate of surplus value at the correct level of abstraction. This is facilitated by considering Morishima's analysis of the issue.[4] Morishima argues thus: under capitalism, the mobility of workers equalizes the length of the working day and equalizes wage rates. Workers, not being tied to capitalists by servile social relations, will move from industries and enterprises where wages are below average and the working day above average length, and this process will continue until a normalization of both remuneration and the working day is achieved. Since wages represent the value of labor power, their equalization standardizes the

---

[4] Michio Morishima, *Marx's Economics* (Cambridge, England: Cambridge University Press, 1972).

value of labor power throughout the economy. The equalization of the length of the working day equalizes the amount of surplus value each worker produces, and the result is an equalized rate of surplus value.

In essence, this argument says that, overall, the societal rate of surplus value is the weighted average of all the rates in each unit of social production, and competition among capitalists for workers tends to reduce the variation around the statistical mean. However, the mean remains derivative from the individual parts. This approach negates the social nature of production under capitalist relations, and, in effect, necessary and surplus labor time are reduced to an issue of measurement. Here there is a confusion between a theory of the equalization of wages and the length of the working day with a theory of the origin of surplus value. Absent is a theory of what determines the level to which wages normalize.[5] When this element is included, as it must be, the order of logic must be reversed, and the societal rate of surplus value established *prior to* considering many capitals.

Morishima's explanation of the equalization of the rate of exploitation is inadequate, first, because it requires a counterfactual assumption of full employment, or at least a relatively small reserve army. If the reserve army is large, capitalists have a pool of unutilized labor power, and the mobility of labor is the mobility from employment to unemployment if workers object to their working conditions and pay. While there are moments when the reserve army is reduced to a low level, this is precisely the moment when the competition among capitals for labor power accentuates and systematically generates differences in wages.[6] The reserve army is reduced in the accumulation process when variable capital is advanced at such a rate to outweigh the ex-

---

[5] Morishima is, of course, aware of Marx's theory of wages, and we are not criticizing him for not considering the value of labor power at all. Our criticism is that he does not use the concept when he comes to derive the rate of surplus value for society as a whole.

[6] See John Weeks, "The Process of Accumulation and the 'Profit Squeeze' Hypothesis," *Science and Society* 43 (Fall 1979).

pelling of living labor from production. In such circumstances, capitalists must bid against one another to obtain labor power for expansion, and the necessary consequences of this is to increase the variance in wages, not to decrease it, as Morishima's explanation requires.[7]

The implicit assumption of full employment equilibrium by Morishima reflects a purely formalistic and mechanistic treatment of wages in capitalist society. The treatment is formalistic in that it is divorced from the process of accumulation, in which wages are capital advanced, not merely income to the working class. In fact, wages are treated as if they were merely one component of the net product, qualitatively no different from profits. A parallel argument could be made for the equalization of the profit rate, so the difference between profits and wages is purely formal, almost semantic, insofar as the equalization of each across industries is concerned.

In order to understand the rate of surplus value, we require a theory that explains the determination of the length of the working day and theory of the wage level. One cannot consider the equalization of either profits or wages across capitals until one has a prior explanation of to what level equalization will gravitate. It could be argued that Morishima implicitly refers to the value of labor power as the basis for the equalization of wages, since he analyzes this elsewhere in his book; but there is no explanation of what determines the working day. In capitalist society, the working day first becomes a period of time defined independently of the direct producer, which confronts him as predetermined. In precapitalist society, when the direct producer is united with means of production, the time of work is determined indirectly, by the need to reproduce the family and to satisfy the demands of the appropriating class for a surplus product of a given size. Under such circumstances, the division of the peasant's life between work and nonwork has little objective meaning,

[7] It is a well-known empirical generalization for industrial capitalist countries that the variance in wage rates among industries increases in periods of "boom" and decreases when accumulation slows or becomes negative.

since work does not present itself as something external to the producer, something out of his control.

The separation of labor from the means of production means that the proletariat can only be reunited with the latter by capital and under the domination of capital. The length of the working day becomes an object of class struggle as the capitalist class attempts to extract as much unpaid labor as possible. The very existence of surplus value requires that the working day extend longer than necessary labor time (the value of labor power). The struggle over the duration of work is a struggle between the two great classes of capitalist society, and in every capitalist country it has been an epochal struggle of the working class.[8]

The struggle over the duration of work has two aspects. As we have seen, capitalist relations create the working day as something distinct from the rest of the worker's life. The basic struggle for the working class is to establish that this working day not be set by the capitalist; i.e., that there be a working day of definite limits set by labor, not capital. Obviously, this struggle takes the form of its second aspect, the limitation of the hours of work. But what is at issue in the struggle is much more profound than a question of time; the struggle is basically over the extent to which capital controls labor. The establishment of a limit to the working day thus reflects an assertion of the collective power of the working class.

The successful struggle by the proletariat to limit the working day is epochal in a second sense, in that by definition it restricts the ability of capitalist to raise surplus value absolutely and ushers in the period of capitalist accumulation when the raising of surplus value relatively is the dominant source of accumulation.[9] What before was a technological possibility—the reduction of necessary labor time by revolutionizing the means of production, which reduces the val-

[8] May Day celebrates a mass mobilization of American workers in Chicago demonstrating for the eight-hour day in the 1880s.

[9] Ben Fine and Laurence Harris, *Re-reading Capital* (New York: Columbia University Press, 1979).

ues of commodities—becomes an objective necessity if surplus value per worker is to be increased. Through an understanding of capitalist relations of production, one can explain why the working day becomes a source of class conflict, but it is not possible to determine the length of the working day theoretically. It is determined in the concrete practice of class struggle, historically by legislation and the fight to ensure that that legislation be enforced. In Marx's famous phrase, "the working day is, therefore, determinable, but is, *per se*, indeterminate."[10] The process by which the working day is equalized across branches of industry, be it by mobility of workers or class struggle, presupposes a process of class conflict at the level of society as a whole.[11]

The length of the working day exists for society as a whole, and variations in particular industries and workplaces are variations of that predetermined level. The same is true for the value of labor power (necessary labor time). In all class societies, total production can be divided conceptually between necessary product and surplus product, where the former is the basis of the reproduction of direct producers and the latter appropriated by the ruling class. In capitalist society, necessary product or necessary labor is valorized. Workers exchange their labor power against money, and exchange money for the means of consumption. Because of this money intermediary, exploitation is veiled under capitalism, as it appears that the wage covers the entire working day; i.e., formally the wage is exchanged for a contracted period of time. Surplus labor and necessary labor are not separated, as they are under feudalism. Despite the illusion that "surplus labor and necessary labor glide one into the other,"[12] their division in capitalist production is as real as in precapitalist society, and wages are merely one historical

---

[10] *Capital*, I, p. 223.

[11] "Hence it is that in the history of capitalist production, the determination of what is a working day, presents itself as the result of a struggle, a struggle between collective capital, i.e., the class of capitalists, and collective labor, i.e., the working class." *Ibid.*, p. 225.

[12] *Ibid.*, p. 227.

form in which the direct producer obtains his means of subsistence. The phenomenal form of the payment to labor,
wages, reflects the value of labor power. The value of labor
power has two components, the collection of use values consumed by workers and the unit values of these use values.

Each of these components is socially determined, and the
particular wages paid in various industries derive from the
socially established norm. That the standard of living is socially determined is obvious. The struggle of the working
class as a whole, in the context of all the complex factors
that tend to divide and unite the class, in combination with
the productivity of labor, set the standard of living. However, it is not primarily the social nature of the standard of
living of the working class that makes the value of labor
power a socialized variable. Given the standard of living, the
labor time necessary to produce the use values that compose
it depends upon the overall development of the productive
forces. Such is not the case under precapitalist relations.
Where producers are self-sufficient, necessary labor is particular to each, a consequence of the fertility of the soil, size of
the family, etc. But under capitalism, necessary labor time is
established independently of the efficiency or inefficiency of
production in any specific branch of industry. Given the
standard of living, the value of labor power is determined by
the social productivity of labor in all branches of industry
that produce consumption commodities and in the branches
that produce the means of production for these consumption
commodities.

To establish a general rate of surplus value by beginning
with the relationship between wages and profits in each industry, as Morishima does, negates the socialized nature of
capitalist production and its complex division of labor. In
effect, it assumes that each worker produces his own means
of subsistence in isolation. In reality, each worker labors and
receives a claim on the total value produced in society. He
then exchanges this claim against a collection of use values
that is the result of the combined, cooperative labor of all

workers (including himself).[13] The rate of surplus value exists first for capital as a whole, since both the working day
and necessary labor time are determined at this level of analysis. This does not deny the existence of differences in
wages, which reflect skill differences, historical particularities, and divisions within the working class. But these differences do not affect the determination of the rate of surplus
value, which arises from the class struggle and the development of the productive forces as a whole.

The foregoing analysis allows us to proceed on the basis
of the abstraction that all workers produce equal amounts of
surplus value, and to employ this abstraction without reference to the particularities of each industry and work process.
What we have established is the socialized nature of exploitation under capitalism in contrast to precapitalist society,
where exploitation is particular and one cannot speak of a
rate of exploitation. Each capitalist exploits his workers to
the extent and degree which capital as a whole exploits the
working class as a whole, an aspect of what Marx called "the
operating fraternity of capitalists."

B. THE RATE OF PROFIT

The social nature of exploitation under capitalism allows us
to consider the function of the rate of profit in capitalist society. The central point to be made is that the role of the rate
of profit in capitalist society is to distribute surplus value
among capitalists and only secondarily has to do with efficiency. In bourgeois theory, variations in the profit rate
among industries indicate allocative efficiency, or "non-op-
tional allocation of resources." But this conclusion is based
upon the illusion that dead labor ("capital" in bourgeois political economy) creates value. By developing the concept of
the average and general rates of profit, we shall demonstrate

---

[13] We are ignoring the production of luxury commodities—those commodities that are neither normally bought by workers nor are inputs into
the commodities workers buy.

the source of this illusion and the distributive role of the rate of profit.

Surplus value is the source of profit and living labor is the creator of surplus value. These basic propositions of the labor theory of value will be taken as given.[14] In order to initiate production—unite labor power with the means of production—capitalists advance money. The historical process by which labor is separated from the means of production dictates that these elements of the forces of production can be set in motion only by the movement of capital. Total capital advanced is composed of variable capital, exchanged for labor power, and constant capital, exchanged for the means of production.

The average rate of profit is the ratio of total surplus value to total capital advanced, constant and variable, for capital as a whole. This average rate of profit, like the rate of surplus value, exists for capital as a whole, behind the backs of capitalists, as the basis of the profit rate in each industry.[15] The conceptual movement from the rate of surplus value to the average rate of profit is a simple algebraic exercise, and this exercise reflects the social relations of capitalist society. Because both the means of production and labor power are set in motion as capital, the profit calculation is on the basis of the sum of these, though only living labor creates surplus value. When the average rate of profit is generalized to all branches of industry as the general rate of profit, the fact that

[14] For a simple explanation, see Ben Fine, *Marx's Capital* (London: Macmillan, 1974), and for a more detailed treatment, *Capital*, I, Chapters VII–IX.

[15] Using the usual notation,

$$\text{the rate of surplus value, } s' = \frac{SV}{V}$$

$$\text{the average rate of profit, } p = \frac{S}{CC + V}$$

$$p = \frac{s'}{\dfrac{C}{VC} + 1}$$

Where C/V is the value composition of capital.

profit is calculated upon capital that is not value creating (but only value transferring) creates the need for a transformation process. Across industries, the ratio of constant to variable capital varies, so if commodities exchanged according to their values, relatively more surplus value would be produced and realized in industries where the ratio of constant to variable capital was low than where it was high. In other words, the rate of profit would vary inversely with the ratio of constant to variable capital, since only the latter creates surplus value. This apparent contradiction gives rise to the transformation problem.

It is important to understand the sense in which there is a problem. The problem is not a conceptual one, but one of capitalist distribution. The basis upon which surplus value is produced is inconsistent with the inherent mobility of capital, which calls forth a general or equalized rate of profit. While considering how this distribution of surplus value is affected by the requirement that the rate of profit be equalized, we must consider the question of efficiency. The efficiency of production in capitalist society is determined by the extent to which any particular capital conforms to the social norm established for the use of concrete labor in the production of its particular commodity or commodities. As explained in Chapter II, this norm is socially necessary abstract labor time (value), and it is established through the interaction of producers. This norm includes both the productive consumption of the means of production and of labor power. Consider the case of two industries, in which all the producers (capitals) in each use the same technique of production, but in one industry the prevailing technique involves a higher ratio of constant to variable capital than the other. If commodities sell at their values, the industries will display different rates of profit. By definition, one is more profitable than the other. However, this greater profitability implies nothing but the fact that the distribution of surplus value does not conform to the distributional requirements of capitalist social relations. The difference in profit rates does not imply that one industry is more efficient in production than the other, nor does it indicate allocative inefficiency. Further, the equalization of the rate of profit has no impact upon the average rate of profit (rate of profit for society as a whole).

That the difference in profitability does not reflect efficiency in the use of the means of production and labor power follows from our assumption that all producers use the same prevailing technique. In this respect, bourgeois theory would concur, since in that theory all producers are always both economically and technically efficient. However, bourgeois theory argues that differences in profit rates reflect allocative inefficiency, since the marginal product of capital is lower in one industry than the other if profit rates differ. On the basis of the labor theory of value, no such argument can be made, for dead labor does not create value or surplus value. One might, however, attempt to salvage the allocative efficiency argument by suggesting that differences in profit rates across industries (which are the result of differences in the ratio of constant to variable capital) indicate that the proportion in which commodities are produced is incorrect, and that the equalization of the rate of profit establishes "correct" proportions. This is an untenable argument, for Sraffa, among many others, has demonstrated that the equalization of the rate of profit across industries is independent of the composition of output.[16] Any distribution of gross output is consistent with an equalized rate of profit, given the technology of production.

We can conclude that the movement of capital to equalize the rate of profit has little to do with productive efficiency nor with allocative efficiency. In capitalist society, reallocations of labor power and the means of production are brought about by the movement of capital, of course. This is because capitalist production is anarchic, and variations in profit rates are the signaling mechanisms to which capital responds. But there is nothing efficient about this method of

[16] As long as all "basic" industries have positive outputs. See P. Sraffa, *The Production of Commodities by Means of Commodities* (Cambridge, England: Cambridge University Press, 1973).

achieving the division of labor. It is merely the particular way in which the division of labor must be achieved in capitalist society.

The point we have made is that differences in profit rates among industries do not indicate any differences in efficiency among those industries so long as one maintains the assumption that the capitals ("firms") in each industry are equally efficient in their productive consumption of labor power and the means of production. On this assumption, the "representative firm" assumption of bourgeois theory, the movement of capital among industries merely redistributes surplus value. The movement of capital acts only to resolve the contradiction between the production of surplus value and the necessity that capital everywhere receive an equal return (as a tendency).

The movements of capital in response to differential profit rates do result in major qualitative changes in a capitalist society, but these movements and their effects are the result of the uneven development of capital in each industry. The theory of the equalization of the rate of profit, which transforms values into prices of production, abstracts from differences among capitals in order to demonstrate the unique relationship between values and prices. Once we move to the level of many capitals and their differences in production techniques, we must consider the centralization and concentration brought about by the movement of capital. These processes are treated in our discussion of competition and fixed capital (Chapters VI and VII).

The law of the equalization of the rate of profit, an aspect of the law of value, is a law of distribution of surplus value among capitalists. It resolves the contradiction that surplus value is produced by living labor, but distributed on the basis of total capital advanced. Since this contradiction arises only under capitalism, the law of the equalization of the rate of profit is relevant only within capitalist relations.

This distribution of surplus value among capitalists generates the illusion that dead labor creates value, which in turn generates the illusion that the movement of capital achieves allocative efficiency. The rate of profit is equalized by an adjustment of values into prices of production.[17] In the process of this adjustment, surplus value is redistributed such that in each branch of the economy a given amount of capital receives the same return, regardless of its composition (ratio of constant to variable capital).[18] Since constant capital commands surplus value in distribution equally with variable capital, this generates the illusion that dead labor is value creating. Bourgeois theory is based upon this illusion. Its analysis is not so much wrong as it is merely a faithful and detailed elaboration of the illusion that arises in circulation. Perhaps there is no better example of the power of Marx's insight that it is the sphere of production that is primary. By starting from the sphere of production, we discover that apparently crucial regulator of capitalist society—the general rate of profit—is merely a distributive algorithm for the "operating fraternity of capitalists."

C. Profit, Value, and Socialist Society

Since the establishment of the first workers' state by the Bolshevik seizure of state power in 1917, a debate has raged over

[17] We shall not deal with the details of the transformation process. See Gerstein, "Production, Circulation and Value," and Fine and Harris, *Rereading Capital*, Chap. 2.

[18] In a two-sector model, this obviously implies that the price of production must rise in the sector where C/V is high and will fall in the other. If this is achieved by the movement of capital, this implies that capital will move from the industry with a high value composition to the industry with a low value composition. This simplified model is what, presumably, has prompted some to say that the labor theory of value "predicts" that industries of low value composition will in general grow faster than ones of high value composition. The critics go on to say that this does not manifest itself empirically, so the labor theory of value is wrong. [See D. Albert and R. Hahnel, *Unorthodox Marxism* (Boston: South End Press, 1978).] The argument cannot be taken too seriously. First it assumes the transformation process must be repeated each time there is an exchange. More technically, Sraffa has shown that in the case of a multisectoral economy, it is not possible to generalize as to what type of price movement will occur in any particular industry. Sraffa, *The Production of Commodities*, Chap. 4.

the extent to which the laws of commodity production continue to be relevant under socialist construction. A major aspect of this debate has been over the role of the law of value during socialist construction.[19] Without treating that debate as such, we can consider the issue on the basis of the foregoing analysis.

Socialism represents the first form of society in which exploitation is abolished (excluding primitive society). Through violent seizure of power, the proletariat, led by its vanguard party, destroys the rule of capital. This implies the elimination of the capitalist class's monopoly on the means of production and, consequently, labor power is no longer a commodity. In effect, labor and the means of labor are reunited by virtue of the expropriation of the property of the capitalist class. This expropriation necessarily implies planning, since the state has seized the means of production in the name of the working class, and they will no longer be set in motion by capital.

In this context, the question arises as to what role, if any, is played by value, which, as we saw, arises because of the private nature of capitalist production. As previously demonstrated, the law of value has two components: (1) it is the law of the minimization of the use of concrete labor in production, and (2) it is the law of the equalization of the rate of profit across industries. Clearly, the second aspect of the law of value loses all relevance in socialist society. The equalization of the rate of profit serves merely to distribute surplus value among capitals in a capitalist society, as argued previously. Since the expropriation of the bourgeoisie eliminates capitalists, this distributive function is no longer necessary, independently of the relevance of the first aspect of the law of value. The equalization of the rate of profit is an objective law only under capitalist relations of production. Even under

---

[19] Stalin, for example, characterized this as an objective law applicable to any society in which products circulate as exchange values. Joseph Stalin, *Economic Problems of Socialism in the USSR* (Peking: Foreign Language Press, 1972), pp. 18-24. This work is treated in the appendix following this chapter.

these social relations it plays a limited role, since total surplus value (and thus total profit) is determined for capital as a whole and is quantitatively unaffected by its distribution among capitals.

The irrelevance of profitability differentials among industries under socialist relations of production is relatively uncontroversial. More contentious is the functioning or nonfunctioning of the first aspect of the law value. To consider the law of the minimization of labor time, let us treat the period of socialist construction during which the means of production have been socialized, so that no significant capitalist ownership remains, though private production may (and usually does) persist in agriculture in the form of peasant land holdings.

In capitalist production, the use of concrete labor in production is minimized by the competition among capitals and the commodity status of the means of production and labor power. That "inputs" are commodities means that they confront the capitalist in money form, and this money form requires that they be reconverted into money form in order that the production process be initiated afresh. The competition among capitals determines the conditions under which these inputs can be reconverted into money. If one capitalist employs the means of production or labor power less economically than average, he will recover less money capital than average when he realizes his commodity capital in the market. A loss or a profit below normal will result, and the less efficient capital will not be able to expand in pace with its fellows.

Under socialist relations, capitalist competition is eliminated, and the means of production and labor power are not commodities, if we ignore for the moment raw materials arising from peasant production. We must consider the implication for the law of value of each of these changes under socialism. Capitalist competition is the consequence of the separation of workers from the means of production, which sets them free in the sense that the allocation of labor is determined by the advancing of capital that requires the mobility of labor.[20] Under socialism, labor power is not a commodity in that workers cannot be hired and fired at will. Employment can become a right guaranteed by the socialist state, because the means of production are no longer the monopoly of the capitalist class. Although workers are shifted between branches of industry, the shift is not based upon private production decisions. The right to employment necessarily implies the elimination of competition. The consequence of competition in capitalist society is that the strong eliminate the weak capitals and expand by virtue of appropriating the labor power of the weaker, declining capitals. This mechanism of the unplanned attrition of capitals is eliminated under socialism. Whatever form competition assumes under socialism (if any), it cannot be the capitalist competition that is part of the law of value. In other words, socialist enterprises cannot fight the "civilized warfare" of price competition, since labor power is not distributed on the basis of free wage labor. The absence of competition reflects the fact that labor power and the means of production cannot be set in motion by advancing money. Private production has been eliminated, in that it is no longer separate, private decisions that bring about the division of labor. Money alone no longer represents a claim upon the forces of production. This does not preclude monetary calculations in socialist enterprise, but these monetary calculations cannot be translated into the conversion of money into the means of production and labor power.

If labor power and the means of production are not commodities, then, by definition, they have no value; they are distributed as use values. Their distribution may involve monetary calculations, but this does not alter the fact that they are distributed as use values, not values. The distinction is not a semantic one, but reflects the nature of two types of social production—capitalist and socialist. Consider first labor power. In socialist society people will be expected to work and even required to do so in order to participate in

---

[20] The theory of competition is considered in Chapter VI.

society's wealth. The requirement that the mass of the population work does not make labor power a commodity; this is a requirement for the reproduction of any society, socialist, capitalist, feudal, etc. In the case of capitalist society, the opportunity to work—to be united with the means of production—is contingent upon the needs of capital. When capital is in crisis, the opportunity to work is systematically denied to a large portion of the masses. This dependence by the proletariat upon capital to unite it with the means of production is not eliminated by decree, but achieved by eliminating production for exchange value. Implied is the conscious planning of production so that production in general and the composition of production is not contingent upon the production of surplus value and its distribution among capitals. Planning prior to production and planned circulation of the products of labor becomes the method by which labor power is freed from its commodity status. This planning requires that the means of production—machinery, intermediate products, raw materials—in the main also not be commodities. Were they commodities, they could be put in motion by money. Since the means of production are useless without labor power, putting the means of production in motion through advancing money would imply the necessity to do the same with labor power.

Here we are speaking of socialist planning, not planning in some abstract sense.[21] Socialist planning is the reflection of class struggle, in which the working class seizes the control of the means of production from the bourgeoisie and asserts its control over the product of its labor and the labor process. This control is achieved in form by the elimination of capitalist private property and in practice through conscious, purposeful planning of the social division of labor. Central to the task of socialist planning is the distribution of the means of production as use values. In effect, this eliminates their existence as capital, since they cannot be bought

[21] That is, we mean planning in the sense Bettelheim uses it in his debate with Sweezy. See Paul M. Sweezy and Charles Bettelheim, *On the Transition to Socialism* (New York: Monthly Review, 1971), pp. 15ff.

or sold. This point can be clarified by considering a society in which the state rather than individuals holds title to the productive enterprises of society, but in which machinery, intermediate products, and raw materials are commodities. That is, they are commodities in that they could be obtained by advancing money. Such a society would be capitalist, and the productive enterprises would be capitalist enterprises. In this society, the means of production would be distributed through markets, so that expansion of enterprises would depend upon the successful repetition of the circuit M-C-M', and, therefore, profitability.

Profitability, in turn, would be determined by competitive pressures; and the competition would be made possible by the commodity status of the means of production. Labor power would in practice if not in form be a commodity, since its employment would have to match the distribution of the means of production. The hypothetical example points up an important distinction. In capitalist society, the monopolization of the means of production by the bourgeoisie takes the form of the ownership of fictitious property, financial representations of the means of production.[22] This fictitious property could be eliminated or assumed by the state, without in principle eliminating capitalism, if the means of production (machinery, intermediate products, raw materials) remained as commodities. What would be altered would be the form of administration of the capitalist economy and society.[23] In such a society a form of planning would occur, since nominally ownership would be centralized in the state. However, such planning could not eliminate the anarchic nature of capitalist production.

In contrast, in socialist planning the means of production and labor power are distributed as use values, and we need to consider the consequences of this for the first aspect of the law of value—the law of the minimization of the use of concrete labor. Since the means of production are not commod-

<hr />

[22] This point is pursued in Chapter VI.

[23] V. I. Lenin, " 'Left-wing' Childishness and the Petty-Bourgeois Mentality," *Selected Works* (Moscow: Progress Publishers, 1970), II.

ities, this leaves only the means of subsistence (products for personal consumption) to circulate as commodities. If the means of subsistence are acquired by the population through the exchange of money for them, then they are formally commodities in that they are exchange values. However, as said in Chapter II, the formality of exchange does not imply that value rules exchange. By a similar argument, it can be shown that value is irrelevant to exchange in socialist society. Since the inputs to the products of socialist enterprises are not values, then the products themselves do not contain abstract labor. Labor power and the means of production enter the production process as use values so that no process of reduction from concrete to abstract labor occurs. There is no process of competition among socialist enterprises by which abstract necessary labor time is generated as an objective reality independent of the production units. The forces of production present themselves in socialist society as what they are—material objects—not in the fetishized form of commodities. In the absence of capitalist competition, exchange is "merely a formal moment," in Marx's phrase.

In our discussion of the operation of socialist society, we have not dealt with the distribution of society's net product—the distribution of income. Instead, we have focused on the social relations within which the means of production and labor power are distributed. As Marx argued in his criticisms of the Gotha Program,[24] the social relations that govern the distribution of society's productive forces also govern the distribution of the social product. Just as in capitalist society the monopolization of the means of production by an exploiting class generates inequality in the distribution of

[24] Karl Marx, *The First International and After* (New York: Vintage Books, 1974), pp. 339-359. "The distribution of the means of consumption at any given time is merely a consequence of the distribution of the conditions of production themselves; the distribution of the latter, however, is a feature of the mode of production. . . . If the material conditions of production were the cooperative property of the workers themselves a different distribution of the means of consumption from that of [capitalism] would follow of its own accord" (p. 348).

wealth and income, so in socialist society non-exploitative social relations of production create the conditions for the eventual elimination of inequality in the distribution of wealth and income.

In summary, the social basis of the law of value—commodity production—is eliminated under socialism. Commodity production is not merely the exchange of products against money but a system in which production units carry out their activities in isolation and achieve a social division of labor through exchange. During socialist construction, this isolation of producing units ends, through the conscious planning of the distribution of the means of production and labor power. Monetary calculations persist, particularly during the early stages of socialist construction, but these monetary calculations do not reflect value, as under capitalism, since the social basis of value formation no longer exists.[25] To the extent that any aspect of the law of value persists during socialist construction, it is evidence of the continued operation of capitalist social relations of production; specifically, the means of production and labor power remain commodities. Following on Marx's insight that the law of value is the law of the appropriation of unpaid labor, we can add that the persistence of the means of production and labor power in commodity form implies exploitation, so the operation of the law of value is the negation of socialist construction.

It must be stressed that we have not argued that the expropriation of the bourgeoisie's property implies necessarily the elimination of the law of value. Assumption by the state of formal titles of ownership of the economic institutions of capitalist society does not in and of itself affect the commodity status of labor power and the means of production. This can be seen in capitalist societies in the behavior of nationalized industries, which remain capitalist enterprises, since

---

[25] We take this to be Bettelheim's point in his sometimes quite cryptic, but path-breaking work on the law of value in socialist society. Charles Bettelheim, *Economic Calculations and Forms of Property* (New York: Monthly Review Press, 1975), pp. 50ff.

labor power and the means of production are produced and distributed as commodities. Socialist transformation requires that the expropriation of the bourgeoisie go beyond the seizure of title to property, on to the process of eliminating commodity production in the means of production and abolishing the buying and selling of labor power. Once these steps are accomplished, the law of value, a law of capitalist accumulation, not a "natural" law, falls into the "dustbin of history."

D. Political Implications of Value Theory

The purpose of these first three chapters has been to demonstrate that the law of value is the law of the exploitation of labor under capitalist social relations. What appears as the law of equal exchange hides the appropriation of surplus value. By developing this theory, Marx could analyze the dynamics of capitalist society and, in particular, crises. In addition, he used his analysis of value as the basis of his political critique of populist critics of capitalism, namely Proudhon. The Proudhonists, and Sismondi before them, argued that commodity production of itself did not give rise to exploitation, but rather commodity production within capitalist social relations. Proudhon himself argued that one could have the former (commodity production) without the latter (capital) by eliminating money, since in his view money was the social vehicle by which wealth was accumulated. In the absence of money, each producer would be able to accumulate no more wealth than he could create by his own working capacity. Therefore, the Proudhonist strategy for the elimination of capitalist exploitation was to return to a society of peasants and craftsmen without wage labor.

Marx demonstrated such a strategy to be a romantic fantasy by showing that commodity production necessarily implied relations of capitalist exploitation insofar as commodity production became general. To return to a situation without capitalist relations of production would be to return to feudalism, slavery, or some other form of class society in which the means of production and labor power are not commodities. The same argument can be made, and was made by Marx, against those who seek to construct a socialist society without eliminating commodity production. The argument that exploitation can be eliminated within a commodity-producing society still has its supporters, the best known variant being the "decentralized market socialism" of Oscar Lange, the Polish economist. Central to these visions of a commodity-producing socialist society is the argument that the central social relation in capitalist society is private ownership of property.

The stress on the form of ownership leads directly to the strategy of a peaceful, nonviolent transition to socialism, via piecemeal takeover of segments of the economy by the state combined with social democratic taxation and expenditure policies to redistribute income and wealth. Western European Communist parties in particular have selected this road to socialist construction. In the United States, where the political left has been less influential historically, an even milder form of this strategy is pursued by the Communist party ("Moscow line") and other social democrats. Much more emphasis is placed upon regulation and control of monopolies, which are seen as the central problem of modern capitalism.

Our development of the analysis of value should show clearly that none of these reforms—state ownership, redistributive policies, or monopoly regulation—implies in itself any step toward socialism and the elimination of exploitation. Exploitation in capitalist society is the result of the commodity status of labor power (and the means of production). Private ownership is not the basis of labor power and the means of production being commodities; quite the reverse is true. Capitalist private property is made possible by the separation of labor from the means of production, and this separation can exist even if property becomes the collective property of the capitalist class.

The truly revolutionary nature of Marx's critique of capitalism lies in his demonstration that exploitation can only be eliminated when the products of labor no longer take the "fantastic" form of commodities. Regulations, redistributions, and nationalizations merely alter the superficial aspects of capitalist society. While the struggle to achieve these reforms certainly plays a significant role in the development of class conflict, they in no way alter the essentially capitalist nature of a society. This essential nature is altered not by piecemeal reforms and tactical limitations on the operation of capital, but by a decisive struggle on the part of the working class to take state power and create a new, socialist state that eliminates commodity production.

Between capitalist and communist society lies a period of revolutionary transformation from one to the other. There is a corresponding period of transition in the political spheres and in this period the state can only take the form of a revolutionary dictatorship of the proletariat.[26]

[26] Marx, *The First International*, p. 355.

APPENDIX

STALIN'S VIEWS
ON THE LAW OF VALUE

In the early 1950s, Joseph Stalin, then leader of the world's leading socialist state, wrote a pamphlet that sought to develop theoretically the nature of commodity production during socialist construction.[1] The pamphlet deals with a number of issues of socialist construction, but we are primarily interested in its discussion of the law of value.

Stalin's view of the law of value in this work is similar to that of Engels, in that he does not see the law as a law of capitalist production:

> Commodity production must not be identified with capitalist production. They are two different things. Capitalist production is the highest form of commodity production. Commodity production leads to capitalism only *if* there is private ownership of the means of production, *if* labor power appears in the market as a commodity, which can be bought by the capitalist and exploited in the process of production.[2]

He adds that the law of value rules exchange whenever there is commodity production. From this, it follows that the law of value operates under socialist relations of production:

> It is sometimes asked whether the law of value exists and operates in our country, under the socialist system. Yes, it does exist and does operate. Whenever commodities and commodity production exist, there the law of value must also exist.[3]

[1] Stalin, *Economic Problems.*   [2] *Ibid.*, p. 14.   [3] *Ibid.*, p. 18.

The difficulty with sorting out what Stalin means by "existence" and "operation" is that he nowhere defines what he means by the law of value, though he indicates clearly that he does not mean the tendency for the rate of profit to equalize across branches of industry.[4] His exclusion of this aspect of the law of value leaves some confusion, however. On the one hand, he takes pains to reject the relevance of any concept of "surplus product" or "surplus labor time" under socialist construction,[5] but on the other hand, he repeatedly refers to the "profitability" of industry.[6] Thus, we can only speculate on the source of profit under socialism. Whatever theory of socialist profit is implicit in Stalin's work, it is not the law of value.

The closest Stalin comes to explaining what he means by the law of value occurs when he discusses its alleged influence in a socialist society. He argues that it performs "the function of a regulator" for "articles of personal consumption."[7] It is restricted to such commodities because, he points out, the means of production are not commodities in the USSR to any great degree. However, even for consumer articles he appears to contradict himself:

> True, the law of value has no regulating function in our socialist production, but it nevertheless influences production, and this fact cannot be ignored when directing production.[8]

It is not obvious how a law serves "within certain limits

[4] "If this were true, it would be incomprehensible why our light industries, which are the most profitable, are not being developed to the utmost, and why preference is given to our heavy industries, which are often less profitable, and sometimes altogether unprofitable." *Ibid.*, p. 22.

[5] "I think we must also discard certain other concepts taken from Marx's *Capital* . . . and artificially applied to our socialist relations. I am referring to such concepts, among others, as 'necessary' and 'surplus' product, 'necessary' and 'surplus' time." *Ibid.*, p. 17.

[6] See footnote 4 and *ibid.*, p. 23, where he speaks of "plants which are more profitable."

[7] *Ibid.*, p. 18.

[8] *Ibid.*, p. 19.

. . . the function of a regulator," but "has no regulating function," only influencing production. Stalin seems to have in mind that socialist managers must consider "such things as cost accounting and profitableness, production costs, prices, etc.," and "our enterprises cannot, and must not, function without taking the law of value into account."[9] One can conclude from this that the reference to costs, etc., means that the law of value continues to operate as the regulator of efficiency (the law of the minimization of use of concrete labor).

However, as we have seen, this function of the law of value involves the reduction of concrete labor to abstract labor, and is the consequence of competition among enterprises and the buying and selling of labor power and the means of production. Yet Stalin argues that these were *not* commodities in the USSR when he was writing.[10] If they were not commodities, then they could not be values, so enterprises could not take value into account. In fact, this is a contradictory argument. On the one hand, the ingredients of production are not values (commodities); on the other, the law of value "operates" and "influences" production. Both positions cannot be correct.

This contradiction in the argument surfaces repeatedly in *Economic Problems*. As we pointed out in Chapter II, the law of value is a law of the social division (allocation) of labor in a society of isolated producers. If it operates during socialist construction, then it operates as an allocator of labor power and the means of production. Yet how can it do so if these are not commodities? Stalin takes both positions within a page. Speaking of "the second phase of communist society," which the USSR will reach in the future, he says:

> As to the distribution of labor, its distribution among the branches of production will be regulated not by the law of value, *which will have ceased* to function by that

[9] *Ibid.*
[10] *Ibid.*, p. 17.

time, but by the growth of society's demand for goods.
[Emphasis added.][11]

Since he is distinguishing that second stage from the present, it must be concluded that he believed that the law of
value did play a contemporary allocative role. This is, of
course, consistent with the statement that the law of value
influences production. However, one cannot be but confused
to read on the next page:

> These comrades forget that the law of value *can be a
> regulator of production only under capitalism*, with private
> ownership of the means of production, and competi-
> tion, anarchy of production and crises of over produc-
> tion.[12]

These directly contradictory statements reflect a confusion
between the economy of time and the particular form it takes
under capitalism. If we substitute "the necessity to distribute
labor time in a purposeful way"[13] for "the law of value" in
Stalin's pamphlet, the contradictions disappear. He begins
correctly and incisively to demonstrate that the social basis
of value has been largely eliminated in the USSR at the time
of his writing; namely, competition has been eliminated because the means of production are no longer commodities
and nor is labor power. This, however, does not eliminate
the need for the means of production and labor power to be
employed efficiently and consistently with the complex in-
put-output requirements of an industrial society. Faced with
this problem, the basic problem of every society, Stalin returns to the law of value, which he previously rejected implicitly. This return is achieved via the essentially metaphysical and tautological argument that the law of value applies
to all commodity production. Without analyzing what com-

[11] *Ibid.*, p. 22.

[12] *Ibid.*, p. 23.

[13] We are paraphrasing Marx, "Economy of time, to this all economy
ultimately reduces itself. Society likewise has to distribute its time in a purposeful way. . . . However, this is essentially different from a measurement
of exchange values (labor or products) by labor time." *Grundrisse*, p. 173.

modity production is, equating it with the law of value is purely a tautology. Once commodity production is itself analyzed, it is discovered that it involves the ingredients of production being commodities, so it occurs only under capitalism.[14]

The confusion in the argument derives from Stalin's view of economic laws and his conception of the objective and subjective. Early in the pamphlet, criticizing those who see economic laws as relative, he characterizes economic laws as follows:

> It is evident that they confuse laws of science, which reflect objective processes in the nature of society, processes which take place independently of the will of man, with the laws which are issued by governments, which are made by the will of man . . .
>
> [T]he laws of economic development, as in the case of natural science, are objective laws, processes of economic development which take place independently of the will of man.[15]

Stalin then compares economic laws to the law of gravity.[16] We have here an important distinction—that between processes that occur independently of their perception by people (the law of gravity, for example) and those which are the result of the conscious action of people. Stalin implicitly places laws of social organization in the second category. However, a law can be objective, in that it is independent of the will of people individually and collectively, yet be purely social in nature. As Marx wrote in a famous passage:

---

[14] In fact, Stalin implicitly recognizes this, arguing that commodity production requires that the means of production be commodities, and therefore, "Value, like the law of value, is a historical category . . ." [ibid., p. 22]. This, however, is contradictory to his view that there is commodity production under slavery and feudalism [ibid., p. 14]. The confusion arises from not distinguishing between exchange as a *formal moment* in distribution and commodity *production*.

[15] *Ibid.*, pp. 2, 3-4.

[16] *Ibid.*, p. 3.

In the social production of their existence, men inevita-
bly enter into definite relations, *which are independent of
their will*, namely relations of production. [Emphasis
added.][17]

Stalin's treatment of economic laws is a further reflection
of his failure to distinguish between the law of economy of
time and the particular form that law takes under capitalism.
The necessity for people to allocate purposefully their time
in production is a universal law of human society (and of the
animal world for that matter), and might be seen as having
the status of a natural law. But the particular way this is
achieved is historically specific, depending upon "the totality
of these relations of production which constitutes the economic structure of society, the real formation, on which
arises a legal and political superstructure."[18]

In essence, Stalin, like Engels before him, fails to distinguish the twofold nature of labor power under capitalism;
that it is both a use value and a value. As a use value (concrete labor) it is unchanged throughout history, always existing in this form and always requiring some form of allocation. Under capitalism, labor power assumes commodity
form in order to effect that allocation by a specific process.
This twofold nature of labor power corresponds to a twofold
nature of "laws" under capitalism. One is universal, common to all societies (the law of economy of time) and the
other particular (the law of value).

The failure to distinguish the twofold nature of labor
power under capitalism, in turn, comes from a circulationist
method. Like Engels, when Stalin periodizes economic life
he does so not primarily upon the basis of modes of production (social relations), but upon the presence or absence of
commodity circulation. Commodity circulation is equated
with the exchange of the products of labor to any degree, no
matter how insignificant quantitatively and qualitatively. In

[17] *A Contribution*, p. 21.
[18] *Ibid.*

such an approach, the social relations of production play no significant analytical role.

In summary, the confusions and internal contradictions in *Economic Problems* derive from considering the law of value as the "law of embodied (concrete) labor," which in the Marxist literature has its ancestry in Engels.

CHAPTER IV

THEORY OF MONEY

A. INTRODUCTION

Capitalist society is the first mode of production in which the reproduction of the class structure of society and society itself requires the circulation of the products of labor as commodities. In this type of society, production is for exchange value, and products must be converted into money. That is, products are commodities, and as commodities they must be continually realized in the form of a universal, exchangeable equivalent. This universal equivalent is, by definition and practice, money. Therefore, the analysis of capitalist society necessarily requires (and implies) a theory of money.

Despite the central role of money in capitalist society, and despite the fact that it was capitalist production that Marx sought to analyze as his life's work, his theory of money has been largely ignored. Even the best treatments of Marxian theory refer to the analysis of money only in passing, leaving the reader to conclude either that Marx had no theory of money, that he had one but it is not relevant to contemporary capitalism, or that it does not differ significantly from the bourgeois theory of money, and therefore does not require separate exposition. The purpose of this and the following chapter is to develop Marx's theory of money and credit, to show how it provides the basis for a critique of the bourgeois theory of money and reveals the contradictions inherent in commodity circulation.

Marx's treatment of money is frequently discarded on the grounds that his analysis assumed a money commodity (gold), or "convertible" money, and since money is no longer convertible, the analysis is largely an anachronism. Below, we show that the convertibility of money was not assumed, but demonstrated as a theoretical conclusion by Marx, a conclusion of general validity. Treating con-

vertibility as an issue of legal or contractual status is an implicit acceptance of the bourgeois theory of money. The
entire history of the development of the bourgeois theory of
money, from the time of Hume, is a history of an analysis
that, step by step, seeks to treat money purely as a facilitator
of exchange. In this analysis, money is artificially separated
from the process of accumulation and from commodity production itself, so that it can be treated as merely a social
convention. The entire bourgeois treatment of money rests
upon the assumption that money itself has no value. Once
one develops the theory of money in the context of capitalism, it becomes clear that it is not Marx's theory that makes
an arbitrary assumption about the nature of money, but
bourgeois theory that does so. In bourgeois theory, the assumption of valueless money (money as a mere symbol) is
absolutely essential, and commodity money undermines that
theory. In Marx's theory, both valueless money and commodity money are treated, allowing for a general theory of
money.

Exchange is older than capitalism, and this fact, as we have
seen, has led some to seek a theory of exchange that is generally applicable to all periods characterized by exchange to
some degree. But no such general theory is possible, since to
formulate it involves ignoring the relations of production
that wholly determine exchange. The same is true of money:
money is older than capitalism, but no general theory of
money applicable to all periods of its use is possible. Any
theory of money necessarily presupposes particular social relations of production. Here we disagree with other writers,
particularly DeBrunhoff,[1] who argue that the theory of
money should be developed for all forms of monetary circulation, prior to considering money in capitalist society. As
we saw in Chapter III, if we abstract from capitalism to seek
"generality," we abstract from the circulation of commodities as capital (M-C-M'). This reduces all commodity circulation to simple commodity circulation (C-M-C). To treat

---

[1] DeBrunhoff argues that Marx developed his theory of money independently of the capitalist mode of production. Her assertion that money cannot

simple commodity circulation as the more general case implies that the circuit of capital is subsumed within simple
commodity circulation. But, as has been shown, the opposite is the case: simple commodity circulation derives from
the circuit of capital. The basic error of seeking a general
theory of money, applicable to all modes of production, is
that such a theory would by definition abstract from all social relations of production. In consequence, such a theory
cannot relate the circulation or noncirculation of money to
the production of commodities. This approach must by its
very method consider only exchange; moreover, it must
treat exchange in isolation from the social relations that create the possibility for exchange. In practice, it is impossible
to abstract from all production relationships, since the consideration of exchange necessarily implies that the exchanging parties hold title to the commodities they sell. Thus, the
error of seeking a general theory of money is analogous to
Engels's error of seeking a general theory of value. The theory is not, in fact, general at all, for it must be implicitly
based upon a society of petty commodity producers (see
Chapters I and II). The theory of money that we elaborate
below is, therefore, not general in the sense of applying to
various modes of production, but general in that it incorporates the various forms of money that appear in capitalist
society: commodity money, paper money, and credit.

B. Commodity Circulation and Commodity Money

Marx's procedure in *Capital* is to begin with a society in
which there is general commodity circulation and production, to leave the particular nature of this society otherwise
unspecified, and to reveal, step by step, that he has necessarily been considering capitalist society from the outset.[2] The

be understood by looking at it in its most complex form (credit) is correct,
but it does not follow that this involves abstracting from capitalism. Su-
zanne DeBrunhoff, *Marx on Money* (New York: Urizen Books, 1976), pp.
19-23.

[2] This revelation should come as no surprise to the reader, since in the
first sentence of *Capital* Marx tells us that he intends to consider capitalist

purpose of proceeding in this manner is to demonstrate that
private property necessarily implies a social system in which
capitalist property is dominant, and that free competition
necessarily generates capitalist competition and with it concentration and centralization of capital. Since it is necessary
to present certain conceptual abstractions such as the commodity, value (thus abstract labor), and money before one
can consider capital and exploitation under capitalist production, it appears that these concepts have been developed independently of capitalist relations of production. This appearance is what prompted Engels to believe, incorrectly,
that Marx's method was "logical-historical"; i.e., that Marx
developed his concepts in logic in the same order as they
present themselves in history.[3] We have seen that Marx's
treatment of value in the first chapter of *Capital* presupposes
capitalist relations of production. Similarly, his discussion of
money is specific to capitalist relations, and elsewhere he
makes this explicit.[4] At this point we use the word "money"

(bourgeois) society from the outset, "The wealth of those societies in which
the capitalist mode of production prevails, presents itself as 'an immense
accumulation of commodities,' its unit being a single commodity. Our investigation must therefore begin with the analysis of a commodity." *Capital*,
I, p. 43.

[3] Friedrich Engels, "Karl Marx, 'A Contribution to the Critique of Political Economy,' " in *A Contribution*, pp. 225ff. Marx rejected the "logical-
historical" method explicitly: "It would therefore be unfeasible and wrong
to let the economic categories follow one another in the same sequence as
that in which they were historically decisive. Their sequence is determined,
rather, by their relation to one another in *modern bourgeois society*, which is
precisely *the opposite* of that which seems to be their natural order or which
corresponds to historical development." *Grundrisse*, p. 107. Emphasis added.

[4] "From the development of the law that price determines the mass of
money in circulation, it follows that presuppositions are here involved
which *by no means apply to all stages of society*; it is absurd, therefore, to take,
for instance, the influx of money from Asia to Rome and its influence on
Roman prices, and simply to put it beside modern commercial conditions."
Marx and Engels, *Selected Correspondence* (Moscow: Progress Publishers,
1965), p. 106. Emphasis added.
We can contrast this to Engels's view, "[T]he introduction of metallic
money brought into operation a series of laws which remain *valid for all*

to mean the universally accepted form of exchange value for a given population of commodity producers. In what follows, we shall deal at length with the question of whether this universal equivalent need be a commodity. The distinction here is between pure symbols of value (e.g., paper notes) and commodity money, where the latter term refers in general to all possible commodity forms which the general equivalent might take. The term "money commodity" refers to the specific commodity that takes the role of money.

Under conditions of commodity production, products circulate as values, which implies that they not only are exchanged but must be exchanged. In the abstract, this exchange can be considered as the exchange of one commodity for another, in which a formal equivalence is established through exchange. In the abstract, this equivalence is purely definitional, reflecting the act of exchange itself, x exchanges for y, so x and y are equivalent in practice. This we can call (following Marx) the "equivalent form of value," in that the value of the commodity x is represented by the commodity y. Standing alone, commodity x cannot express its value, since it is a material object with certain natural properties, the result of concrete labor. Its value appears as a certain quantity of the commodity y.[5] The property of the commodity y, that it is a use value, is unaffected by virtue of it playing this measurement role. If the commodities are wheat and iron, and they exchange on the basis of one ton of wheat for 100 pounds of iron, then the value of a ton of wheat is this finite quantity of iron. From this point of view, that of the exchange of wheat, the value of iron is unexpressed. In other words, concrete labor, the use value form of the equivalent commodity becomes the value form of the first com-

countries and historical epochs in which metallic money is a medium of exchange." _Anti-Duhring_, p. 187. Emphasis added.

[5] "The body of the commodity that serves as the equivalent, figures as the materialization of human labor in the abstract, and is at the same time the product of some specifically useful concrete labor. The concrete labor becomes, therefore, the medium for expressing abstract human labor." _Capital_, I, p. 64.

modity.[6] This is not a play on words, but expresses the fact that one commodity becomes the value representation of the other. If we bring more commodities into exchange, and they all exchange against the commodity y (iron), then the value of each is expressed as a certain quantity of y (of iron), and y becomes a general equivalent. The fact that iron comes to play this function in our abstract example in no way affects the fact that iron itself has value, but the value of iron is only expressed as a certain amount of the other particular commodities.

In the development of a general equivalent, the abstract labor in each commodity is quantitatively expressed as a weight or volume of the equivalent commodity. The units in which the equivalent commodity are measured are the calibration of the price of those commodities. As the use of this particular commodity as the measure of value generalizes, it appears that this commodity itself has no price, since, by convention, it is the measure of price. The price of the equivalent commodity is hidden by the fact that, due to common usage as an equivalent, its price is subsumed in itself. This is merely to say that the general equivalent cannot measure itself, anymore than any other single commodity can express its own value. By becoming the general equivalent, a commodity becomes functionally isolated from other commodities, so it stands alone as the representation of all other commodities.

The particular natural properties of gold and silver uniquely suit these commodities to the role of universal equivalent.[7] When its use as the universal equivalent is established, the commodity in question, now the money commodity, undergoes a profound change. Its use value becomes its ability to represent abstract labor in general. While it also has an intrinsic use value—iron for example—this becomes obscured, so it appears that its only use is as the representation of the

---

[6] "Hence, the second peculiarity of the equivalent form is, that concrete labor becomes the form under which its opposite, abstract human labor, manifests itself." *Ibid.*, p. 64.

[7] *A Contribution*, pp. 153-157.

value of all other commodities. The process of exchange results in the complete abstraction from the intrinsic properties
of the money commodity. It now appears that the money
commodity has no independent use value, since commodity
producers seek it not for any useful purpose arising from its
natural properties. This allows for the illusion that the
money commodity itself is selected arbitrarily, and that its
value is irrelevant to its role as money. This illusion is vali-
dated in the eyes of commodity producers when the state
issues representations of the money commodity to circulate
in its stead.

The illusion is merely illusion, however. The reality is that
commodities exchange against commodities, and in this
process one commodity establishes itself as a general equivalent. When this happens, its use value in practice is that it
is exchange value, but the fact remains that it is the result of
human labor and a commodity, not merely a valueless convention.

C. Circulation and the Functions of Money

The idea that money need not have value derives from considering it only as a medium of exchange, which, in effect,
treats all exchanges as barter. This can be demonstrated
through a consideration of the process of circulation. We
have implicitly been dealing with capitalism in our abstract
discussion, since it assumed commodity production and the
formation of abstract necessary labor. When we speak of exchange of commodities, we do so in the context of the circulation of commodities, in which a particular exchange is
merely a conceptually isolated moment. Every exchange of
a commodity for the money commodity is part of an endless
series of exchanges. Any exchange taken in isolation appears
as barter and can be so analyzed even when the money commodity is involved.

Consider the case where gold circulates directly as the
money commodity. Since both gold and wheat, say, are the
products of human labor, one could view their exchange as

bartering a quantity of one for a quantity of the other. Alternatively, if representations of gold circulate, and a commodity producer sells wheat for tokens of money, then uses these tokens to buy a book, say, barter exchange can again be imposed upon the process. One could argue that since only a representation of gold was involved, this representation is also a representation of wheat and a book, a mere "veil," as the classical economists called money, which hides the barter nature of the exchange. Both of these analytical methods involve isolating exchange from circulation. The first, which treats the money commodity like any other (direct barter of gold and wheat), implies the second. If the money commodity is like any other, then it plays no distinctive role, and money is merely a convention agreed upon by commodity producers.[8]

The mistake in such an approach is revealed when we locate each exchange as part of an interrelated process of commodity circulation. To consider the circulation of commodities, we must return to the point in the analysis where we demonstrated that commodity circulation is the social mechanism by which isolated producers are integrated into a system of social production. This implies that price (the denomination of value in units of the money commodity) is the form of value, but not equal to value, except momentarily. As we have seen, each capitalist producer marshals the means of production and labor power by advancing money. The price each receives for his commodity is the signal to him of the extent to which he has consumed his productive capital in line with average efficiency. If, overall, the capitals in an industry produce in a manner such that the prevailing demand conditions allow a rate of profit greater than that in other industries, this stimulates the inflow of capital. In such a case, price is greater than value, in that the abstract labor realized in exchange in the form of the money commodity

---

[8] "But if [exchange] is separated from the process [of circulation], the phase C-M [commodities for money] disappears and there remain only two commodities which confront each other, for instance iron and gold, whose exchange is not a distinct part of the cycle but is direct barter." *Ibid.*, p. 90.

exceeds the abstract labor embodied in the commodity in production.[9] The deviation of price from value is a necessary inequality in capitalist production in order that labor and the means of production be constantly redistributed. Thus value must appear in a form in which that form itself allows for a quantitative divergence of value from exchange value. Labor time itself cannot be the calibration of value, since this would not allow for the necessary divergence.[10] The price form arises from the necessary contradiction between value and exchange value. If value is to determine exchange value, then the two must diverge (otherwise it is not a question of determination, but identity). The denomination of all commodities in terms of a generally equivalent commodity is the vehicle for this divergence.

The particular role money plays in this divergence can be demonstrated by use of a simple identity. If commodities exchange at value, the price (money form) of some commodity i is

$$P_i = \alpha V_i,$$

where P_i is the price of the commodity measured in monetary units, α is the number of monetary units per unit of labor time, and V_i is the value of the commodity. This formulation abstracts from the transformation process, so exchange at value is treated as the set of equilibrium relative values. To allow for divergence of relative prices from relative values, we must be precise in our use of the term "exchange value," which is the abstract labor time that a commodity realizes in exchange,

---

[9] This abstracts from the transformation process, an abstraction which does not affect the analysis. The deviation of price from value in order to achieve an equalization of profit rates is considered below.

[10] "Because price is not equal to value, therefore the value-determining element—labor time—cannot be the element in which prices are expressed, because labor time would then have to express itself simultaneously as the determining and the non-determining element, as the equivalent and non-equivalent of itself." *Grundrisse*, p. 140. Marx makes the same point in *The Poverty of Philosophy*.

$$X_i = B_i V_i,$$

where B_i is the index of the deviation of exchange value from price and is different for each commodity. Since all value has a material form (use value form) and only what is produced can circulate, the weighted sum of the B's for all commodities is unity; what one commodity producer loses in exchange, another gains, since every sale is a purchase. Price is the monetary denomination of exchange value, so we can write, as the general case

$$P_i = \alpha B_i V_i,$$

where $P_i = \alpha X_i$, by definition. The value of the commodity is a definite quantity of abstract labor and the B term a distributional parameter determined by the deviation of exchange value from value. The issue to be considered is what determines α, which represents the conversion of labor time into monetary units. It was Marx's argument that α represents the value of the money commodity (or more precisely, the inverse of this). If money has value, then the conversion from labor time to monetary units is unique, and the absolute price of the commodity i is determined by the value of the money commodity.

But can α be purely arbitrary, not tied to any commodity? First, it should be noted that the calibration of price can be arbitrary even with a money commodity. In the case of gold, it can be measured in various physical units and these units can be assigned different arbitrary monetary calibrations (dollars, pounds, yen, etc.). We are not interested in this aspect, but in the question of the necessity of a money commodity, and the two issues must not be confused. The money commodity provides a theory of the absolute price level with relative values given, and a theory that rejects the necessity of a money commodity must provide an alternative explanation of the price level (the determination of α). In bourgeois monetary theory this is provided by the quantity theory of money. In this theory, the parameter α is uniquely determined by the quantity of the medium of exchange in circulation, and Marx's theory of the necessity of a money commodity provides a critique of this theory.

The quantity theory of money treats as exogenous to circulation the supply of money. This concept of the supply of money presupposes what it seeks to establish, that money has no value, since it is presumed that all of the medium of circulation available actually circulates.[11] If all of the medium of circulation does not circulate, then the velocity of money is indeterminate, and the parameter α is indeterminate. That all of the means of circulation in fact circulates is based on the assumption that money has no value, since this assumption allows one to argue that no one would seek to hold money for itself. The argument is, indeed, purely circular: money is a mere convention, having no value; thus there is no motivation to hold money out of circulation; all money therefore circulates; the price level is determined by the amount of money in circulation; and since all money circulates, money must have no value.

This theory considers money to have only one function, as a means of circulation, i.e., that it merely facilitates exchange. However, money must also be a standard of value and a store of value. As a standard of value, it must provide a unique calibration of price that implies a determinant price level. As we have seen, a money commodity serves this function simply, in that its bodily form is the price form, while the valueless-money theory requires a determinant supply of money to satisfy indirectly this function. In the case of valueless money, the crucial concept is the supply of money and its uniqueness. Ignored in this concept is that money serves as a store of value, the form in which a claim on social labor can be accumulated in a capitalist society. It

[handwritten marginal note: unit of account]

---

[11] Sophisticated elaborations of the "pure" quantity theory that include the possibility of holding money for speculative ("liquidity preference") and other reasons does not change this presumption, but merely introduces the interest rate as a mechanism for uniquely determining the "supply of money."

is not accidental that this function is ignored, since by definition, hoarded money does not appear in circulation.[12]

In the circuit of capital, capitalists advance money for commodities (labor power and the means of production), marshal these commodities in production to produce a new set of commodities, then realize these commodities in money form. This circuit of capital can be summarized in symbols,

$$M\text{-}C \ldots P \ldots C'\text{-}M',$$

where M stands for money, C for commodities, and P for the moment of production. The primes indicate a quantitative expansion of value ($C' > C$, $M' > M$). The first exchange, $M\text{-}C$, leaves the capitalist with a collection of commodities that are useless unless employed in production. Similarly, the second exchange, $C'\text{-}M'$, is necessary in order to realize the value and surplus value produced. Since production is for exchange value, neither C nor C' is an adequate form in which to hold capital. Formally, the subsequent conversion of M' into productive capital seems a simple extension of the circulation of capital. However, it is in the initiation of a subsequent circuit of capital in which hoarding or the storing of value occurs. Formally, capital can be held or hoarded as commodities (C or C'), but hoarding in this form requires conversion of the commodities into money before the circuit can be renewed. Money, the general equivalent, is realized capital and can be exchanged against any commodity. What differentiates money from commodities in general is that it need not be realized, since it represents abstract labor in general. However, if money has no value, is not a commodity, then its worth—what it can command in exchange—cannot be predicted nor depended upon. If money has no value, then hoarding by capitalists in money form becomes problematical, and hoarding must occur in the form of specific commodities, not a general equivalent. In fact, legal attempts to cut representations

---

[12] "As a means of circulation money therefore appears always as a *means of purchase*, and this obscures the fact that it fulfills different functions in the antithetical phases of the metamorphosis of commodities." *A Contribution*, p. 98.

of money off from the money commodity (nonconvertibility) result in a run on commodity markets when circulation of capital encounters difficulties, which generates widespread hoarding.

Marx observed that money is always convertible, in practice if not in law.[13] By this he meant that the circuit of capital necessarily involves hoarding, the holding of wealth in a store, and that valueless money is inadequate for this function precisely because it is valueless. Thus we can see that a period of inflation is not empirical evidence of the intrinsically valueless nature of money, but exactly the opposite: the depreciation of representations of money (such as paper money) demonstrates the consequence of attempts by the state to repeal the basic law that money must be a commodity. If the value of the money commodity does not rise, then inflation reflects the quantitative inconsistency between the expansion of representations of money and the performance of social labor (production of value).

The basic difference between Marx's theory of money and the bourgeois theory of money is epitomized in a further function of money that we have yet to consider: money as means of payment. Indeed, this function of money does not appear at all in bourgeois theory or, if it does, only as a triviality. In capitalist society, most transactions are not made with specie, but on the basis of contracting indebtedness (i.e., credit), which involves a promise to repay these debts in the future. Obviously such an arrangement involves a separation in time between purchase and payment, an uncontroversial point. What is controversial is the significance of this separation. If money is valueless, then the separation is trivial, involving the use of one form of valueless money at purchase (credit) and another form of valueless money to cancel the debt. However, in Marx's theory, this separation is of paramount importance because the form of money adequate for purchase is not in general satisfactory for payment. If the separation between purchase and payment cor-

[13] *Ibid.*

responds to a period during which the value that money commands changes, then the conditions under which payment is made are different from the conditions under which purchase was made. The full implications of the separation of purchase and payment will be explored in the next chapter; for the moment, we note that the intervention of money into exchanges does not merely facilitate exchange but creates a system in which commodities may circulate without being paid for.

We have now considered several functions or roles of money, and the central point is that these are not merely different functions of the same thing; i.e., we should not see money as analogous to a tool, such as a hammer, which can be adequately shifted among different uses. Rather, these functions imply different things. As a medium of circulation, money can be a mere symbol, even an agreement to pay among capitalists. As a store of value or a means of payment, it must assume a form in which its relationship to socialized labor can be maintained. A contradiction arises here, since the form of money generated by the circulation of commodities cannot in general satisfy the other functions of money.

D. Marx's "Pure" Theory
of Money and Circulation

The hoarding function requires that the general equivalent be a commodity. This, in fact, is a demonstration that our discussion in Section B, although abstract, established a general point that holds at all levels of abstraction. There we argued that money is a commodity whose use value and value become obscured by virtue of its serving as the embodiment of exchange value. Treating money as valueless is to accept this obfuscation as material fact. The general conclusion that money must be a commodity does not, of course, preclude moments or periods when representations of money are divorced from the money commodity. Such moments or periods do not invalidate the general conclusion, any more than price deviating from value invalidates the law that value is the basis of price. Such moments represent complications—the complexity of the concrete—which are understood by first considering money in its simplest form—gold, for example. It is for this reason that Marx develops his theory of money abstracting from all the complicated developments of the money form—tokens of money, paper money, etc. Money is not assumed to be gold; rather, by beginning at this simple level, the development of the more complex forms will be explained, and we can establish the laws governing them. The simple concept will reveal the complex and concrete, as a logical development of the analysis.[14]

Thus, we begin our analysis of money with the abstraction that gold serves as the medium of exchange. In this case, the parameter α, which we introduced in the previous section, is the inverse of the value of gold. Given the values of all other commodities, the price level rises and falls with increases and decreases in the productivity of gold production. We must investigate the consequences of a change in the supply of gold, with its value given. That is, does an increase in the production of gold, and thus its availability, affect the general level of gold-denominated prices? Here we refer to what Shaikh calls a "pure supply effect," uncomplicated by any change in values of gold or other commodities.[15] It would seem that an increase in the production or availability of gold would give rise to a scenario similar to that predicted by the quantity theory: the increased availability of gold means that there is more gold to exchange against all other commodities, and this excess supply of gold would drive the price of gold down (prices of other commodities up), until

[14] *Grundrisse*, pp. 105-108.

[15] Anwar Shaikh, "On the Laws of International Exchange," *Science and Society* 43 (Fall 1979). Marx comments, "Any scholarly investigation of the relation between the volume of means of circulation and movements in commodity prices must assume that the value of the monetary material be given. . . . It is, of course, quite possible to increase the supply of precious metals while their costs of production remain unchanged. On the other hand a decrease in their value . . . will in the first place be attested only by an increase in their supply." *A Contribution*, p. 160.

all gold was sold. In this line of argument an increased availability of gold has the same consequence as an excess supply
of any other commodity. Thus it would seem that the quantity theory holds for commodity money. Ricardo argued
quite similarly in developing the monetary adjustment mechanism for his theory of comparative advantage.[16] Before considering the basic mistake in this argument, it should be
pointed out that even if an increase in the availability of gold
were to depress its price,[17] the price level that resulted would
not be sustainable. If gold exchanged at its price of production before the increased availability, then the subsequent
higher price level would imply that gold exchanged below
its price of production. This would mean that gold producers
would realize a rate of profit below the general rate of profit,
and capital would move out of gold production, reducing
the relative availability of gold until the original absolute
gold prices were re-established. We can conclude that the use
of commodity money necessarily implies a unique absolute
price level, given the value of the money commodity.

It can be further demonstrated that an increase in the availability of gold would in general not lead to a rise in commodity prices even as a momentary disequilibrium. While
money must be a commodity, the money commodity cannot
be treated as if it were like all other commodities, which the
above argument does. The money commodity differs from
all other commodities in that it need not be realized, since it
is the general equivalent.[18] All other commodities must be
converted into money in order that the circuit of capital be

[16] Shaikh, "On the Laws of International Exchange."

[17] Strictly speaking, gold does not have a price in this context, since it is
itself the denomination of price. It only has an exchange value relative to
any other particular commodity.

[18] Consider the circuit of capital from the point of view of the producers
of all but the money commodity. Their circuit has three moments, M-C
$\ldots P \ldots C'$-M', capital advanced (M-C), the moment of production (P),
and the moment of realization (C'-M'). The producer of the money commodity has no realization moment, M-$C \ldots P \ldots C'$-M'. For the producer
of the money commodity there can be no problem of realization, since
money *is* realized abstract labor.

renewed. If an excess supply of one of these commodities exists, then either the price of the commodity must fall in order to sell the excess or part of value and surplus value is unrealized and remains in a form in which it is useless to the capitalist. Not so with the money commodity.

All producers must convert their commodities into money; money, however, need not be converted into commodities, but can be held as the general embodiment of socialized wealth. The money commodity is a commodity "of its own type," the commodity into which all others must be converted in the circuit of commodities and capital. Thus, the circulation of money is stimulated by the need to realize the nonmoney commodities, and it is drawn into circulation or lies idle depending upon the number and value of commodities to be realized. If for some reason the production of commodities declines (a slow-down in accumulation of capital), money falls out of circulation, accumulates in hoards, as a preserve of value and wealth. In the simple (abstract) case of gold as money, such moments are precisely when commodity prices fall, and the value of money rises. When all other commodities are depreciated due to the necessity of their realization, this is precisely when hoarding is most attractive to capitalists. When accumulation accelerates, these hoards are reduced, as more money is required as means of circulation. In summary, the money commodity differs from all others in that it can be held without its value depreciating.

Precisely because the money commodity is the general equivalent, it plays a passive role in circulation. The basic error of the quantity theory is to assume that all money must circulate. This assumption derives from one of two mistakes, mentioned before. If the money commodity is treated like all others, then like all others it must be realized and cannot be dormant in hoards. If money is assumed to be valueless, then there is no motivation to hoard, since money cannot serve as an adequate preserver of value. Both of these mistakes arise from considering commodity circulation as mere isolated exchange, in which money serves simply as a medium of circulation. Once exchange is placed in the context of circulation, and the circulation of capital, the preserving of value becomes a necessary function, and the movement of commodities is shown to determine the movement of money, not the reverse. "[F]or a given interval of time during the process of circulation, we have the following relation: the quantity of money functioning as the circulating medium is equal to the sum of the prices of the commodities divided by the number of moves made by coins of the same denomination. This law holds generally."[19]

In other words, the circulation of money is passive, determined by the quantity of commodities to be realized and their values.[20] By passive, we mean that money circulates in response to the circulation of commodities. Additional money is drawn into the circuit of capital as a result of an increase in the number and value of commodities to be realized. When we consider interruptions in the circuit of capital, we will argue that the availability of money in a particular form becomes of paramount importance, but this will not amend the general relationship in which the circulation of money derives from the circulation of commodities. We can now summarize Marx's theory of money for the simple case of the direct circulation of commodity money. In the process of production a certain mass of commodities is produced. The social interaction of producers establishes abstract necessary labor time, which is the total value to be realized. These commodities must be thrown into circulation and realized as money. The total amount of money drawn into circulation is determined by this total value and the frequency with which money turns over in a given period of time, where the latter, the velocity of money, is determined by institutional factors, geography, etc. Money not in circulation serves as a store of value. Finally, this implies that

---

[19] *Capital*, I, p. 121.

[20] "Prices are thus high or low not because more or less money is in circulation, but there is more or less money in circulation because prices are high or low. This is one of the principal economic laws." *A Contribution*, pp. 105–106.

the absolute prices are set by the value of the money commodity.

This summary requires one further comment or question. Is it not possible that the money held in hoards would at some points be insufficient quantitatively to circulate the value of commodities? In principle, one can conceive of accumulation proceeding at such a pace that all of the money commodity is drawn into circulation. At this point it would appear that the availability of money would place a brake on accumulation, and more commodities could be circulated only if the exchange value of money fell, in which case absolute prices would no longer be determined by the value of money, or if the velocity of money rose. Here we are no longer considering the circulation of money as such, but the circulation of money in the context of accumulation. We consider this question in the following chapter, where accumulation and money are interrelated. The question here is whether the availability of money can limit accumulation, and no satisfactory answer can be given by analyzing money in the absence of a theory of accumulation.

E. Representations of Money

We have considered four functions of money in the process of the circulation of capital: as a medium of circulation, a standard of value, a store of value, and a means of payment. The commodity nature of money asserts itself in the last three functions and is obscured in the first. As a medium of circulation, money merely facilitates exchange by providing a general intermediary form that abstract labor can assume between exchanges. In exchange, money is merely a symbol, a representation of the value of commodities in general form. As a store of value, it is not merely a symbol of abstract labor, but value itself in its most adequate (liquid) form.

When money acts as a mere symbol, it can be replaced by a symbol itself. The intermediary role of money does not require the physical presence of the money commodity, since the simple act of exchange involves only a standardized cal-

ibration of price.[21] The substitution of the representations of
the money commodity for the money commodity itself reflects this symbolic role money plays in exchange. When the
money commodity falls out of circulation in favor of its
symbolic representations, this does not imply that money
need not be a commodity, but is the functional division of
two roles of money: as a means of circulation (wherein a
pure symbol will suffice) and a store of value (which must
involve commodity money, "money as such," to assure
against devaluation of the store).

The use of symbols of money is a convenience in exchange, since commodity money is bulky and loses weight
in use. But this convenience does not prompt its use, but
presupposes actions by the state to give this convenience social endorsement. A symbol becomes generally accepted
through some social process. In the case of exchange among
independent commodity producers, this process cannot be a
spontaneous one, since competition induces each producer to
extract maximum advantage in exchange. Without state regulation, money would have to be commodity money in order that each producer be assured of its worth, independently
of the good will of other producers.[22] Thus, the issuance of
coins, tokens and paper money involves the intervention of
the state, as the state becomes the guarantor of the worth of
these symbols. This guarantee is maintained by a legal promise of convertibility into the money commodity. In its most
rigid form this convertibility is achieved by limiting the issuance of symbols of money to the amount of the money
commodity available for conversion. In this case, the circulation of symbols of money can be considered analytically
identical to the circulation of gold itself.

However, the intervention of the state in issuing symbols
of money qualitatively alters the analysis since there is no

---

[21] *Grundrisse*, pp. 143-144.

[22] In the United States up to the early part of the nineteenth century,
symbols of money were issued privately (by banks). Such a system depended upon the financial viability of each bank and tended to break down
in periods of economic crisis.

economic law that necessarily limits the amount of currency issued by the state to the amount of available gold. Further, the moment when capitalists generally may wish to store value—during economic crises—is precisely when the state may be unable to convert all symbols to gold. This is particularly true when capitalists hold the currency issued by a foreign state, over which they have limited influence. The issuance of currency represents an integration of the economic and political spheres, and convertibility can be one weapon in the struggle among national capitalist classes. In consequence, the development of symbols of money creates a separation between domestic and international exchange, so that what can serve as a satisfactory medium of circulation within a country may be unacceptable between capitalists of different countries. This is one aspect of the assertion of the necessity of a money commodity, and a symbol of money can circulate internationally only if national capitalist classes join to create a supranational institution to assure the worth of the international medium of exchange.

Before considering the role of symbolic money further, we must deal with two side issues. Foley has argued that commodity money is unnecessary in capitalist circulation, since capitalists (and those of other classes) can carry out exchange on the basis of "promises to pay," i.e., contract indebtedness among themselves.[23] This argument sees the exchanging medium as arising spontaneously in the act of exchange, which we have rejected on the grounds that the competition among capitals would result in repeated breakdowns in such spontaneous agreements. There is a more basic objection to the view that exchange can be based upon promises among commodity producers. Such promises presuppose a nomenclature of price, so that the promises are denominated in standard units. While one can imagine a group of producers spontaneously creating indebtedness among themselves, it is absurd to imagine them sponta-

---

[23] This argument was presented by Duncan Foley in a lecture to the Economics Society of the Department of Economics, American University (Washington, D.C.) April 1980.

neously creating a common nomenclature of prices. Thus, we must have an explanation of the source of the units in which commodity producers calculate their promises. Presupposed here is a standard of value, i.e., the prior existence (both historically and theoretically) of a money commodity that is the basis of monetary calculation. It is a fact that capitalists in a developed capitalist society do carry out exchanges on the basis of promises; however, this method of facilitating exchange cannot be divorced from the historical and social bases upon which such promises have validity. The spontaneous and individual exchange relations that "promises to pay" represent are made possible by the development and sophistication of the credit system. To begin the analysis of money with one of the most developed forms which the medium of circulation assumes is to presume that capitalism initiates its existence in its most developed stage.

The second issue we must briefly consider is the sense in which the state can guarantee and regulate symbolic money. It might be argued that by asserting its monopoly over the issuance of money, the state can render commodity money unnecessary.[24] Involved here are two issues: first, the process of the socialization of credit, which we consider in the next chapter, and, second, the extent of the state's control over the relationship between symbolic money and the circulation of value. It is the second issue that is relevant to the role of commodity money. Both issues require an analysis of credit in order to be resolved. However, at this point we can point out that, if the state seeks to establish a monopoly over the issuance of the means of circulation, this does not eliminate the need for capitalists at certain times to convert symbols of money into commodity money, but merely centralizes in the state the convertibility function.

The issuance of symbols of money creates the possibility of symbols of money being greater than the available quantity of the money commodity, and the law regulating the

[24] The following discussion was stimulated by comments by Mike Williams of Brunel University (United Kingdom).

circulation of worthless symbols of money differs from the laws of the circulation of commodity money. In order to understand the consequence of variations in the availability of currency, we must review the process of circulation in the context of commodity money. Capitalists advance money for labor power and the means of production, and this advance of money is the process by which previously produced means of production and articles of consumption are realized.[25] Production occurs, which establishes the mass of commodities to be realized at the end of the production period. If total value produced increases compared to the previous production period, additional money is drawn into circulation for the requirements of realization (hoards are reduced). The amount of the money commodity serving as a means of circulation expands and contracts, depending on the tempo of accumulation.[26] The circulation of commodities is the basis and motivation for the circulation of money. This implies that a "pure" increase in the availability of money (i.e., an increase with no change in the value of money) results in increased hoarding. In a society of commodity producers, commodities must be transformed into money. If for some reason, all commodities are not transformed into money, this by definition appears as the excess of all commodities compared to the money commodity, i.e., the money commodity appears in shortage. It is a short step to the erroneous conclusion that commodities failed to be realized because of a shortage of the money commodity.[27] This view presupposes what it seeks to establish, namely that all money circulates, that therefore there are no hoards of money to be drawn upon nor motivation to increase them.

[25] The advance of money as constant capital realizes the means of production, and the variable capital, through the hands of the working class, realizes the articles of consumption. *Capital*, II, Chapters XX and XXI.

[26] *Ibid.*, Chapter XVII.

[27] "The movement and changing forms of the circulating commodities thus appear as the movement of money mediating the exchange of commodities . . . The movement of the circulation process is therefore represented by the movement of money . . . i.e., by the *circulation of money*." *A Contribution*, pp. 100-101.

The general use of paper money—valueless money—endorses this quantity-theory illusion, since paper money serves primarily as a means of circulation. Representations of money (by definition valueless themselves) represent a claim on commodities (social labor), but this claim is limited by the amount of value that can be realized, not by the volume of currency itself. If the quantity of currency exceeds the value of commodities (including the money commodity), and capitalists attempt to convert their potential claims on value (nominal claims) into real claims (commodities themselves), then the consequence is a rise in prices denominated in units of the valueless currency. This process can continue until all of the valueless currency is absorbed in circulation.[28]

It appears that the introduction of valueless currency, even if convertible in law, has salvaged the quantity theory of money, since the quantity of currency affects the nominal price level in a more or less proportionate way. However, it is a limited salvage operation, for the bourgeois theory of money is not merely a theory of the price level. What we have argued is that increases in the supply of currency tend to flow into circulation, since representations of money are inadequate as a store of value. Since these tokens of money are representations of something material (commodity money), the claim they represent declines in real terms as their circulation increases beyond the value that has been produced. In other words, their symbolic nature asserts itself; the contradiction inherent in them, that they represent money but are not themselves money, is manifested in their depreciation. Thus the depreciation of currency due to the increase of its quantity is not a theory of the price level, but merely a recognition of the distinction between the real and the symbolic. No theoretical insight is required to predict a rise in nominal prices when the symbolic comes into quantitative contradiction with the real. The theoretical insight begins

[28] "The circulation process will, on the other hand, absorb or as it were digest any number of paper notes, since irrespective of the gold title borne by the token of value when entering circulation, it is compressed to a token of the quantity of gold which could circulate instead." *Ibid.*, p. 121.

when one moves to analyze the consequence of this contradiction upon the material process of the production and circulation of value.

Because the real basis of circulation is commodity money, the excess supply of tokens of money has no consequence but a change in the calibration of price.[29] Variations in the supply of tokens of money do not affect the fact that x amount of gold (the money commodity) exchanges against y amount of iron, but only changes the symbolic representation of iron in terms of gold. The production of commodities determines total value and the productive utilization of labor power and the means of production. More or less paper money in and of itself does not affect this, having no direct impact upon employment, production or the mass of commodities that circulate. Indirect consequences may occur, and these are considered in the next chapter.

We can contrast this to the analysis that follows from the bourgeois theory of money. In this analysis, an increase in paper money flows into circulation. If there be less than full employment, the price level rises more than the money wage, stimulating increased output,[30] and output increases until full employment is reached; if the supply of paper money continues to increase, all prices and wages rise proportionally to the increase in the supply of paper money. Increases in the availability of valueless money stimulates the real variables in the economy, to the extent to which these are not at their maximum values. The bourgeois theory of valueless money is thus not primarily a theory of the price

---

[29] *Ibid.*, p. 122. We are abstracting from the division of capital into money capital and productive capital, which implies the functional division between money capitalists and industrial capitalists. The expansion and contraction of symbols of money can affect the division of surplus value between the two. This is considered in the following chapter, where we treat interest-bearing capital.

[30] The "real wage" falls, leaving the level of employment suboptimal. Whether one considers the pure quantity theory, where the money supply has no effect on savings and investment or the Keynesian variation is of no analytical consequence, except in the case of the liquidity trap. In both cases, increases in the money in circulation stimulate increases in output.

level, but a theory of how the symbolic determines the material.

Marx's theory of money provides a critique of this analysis by demonstrating that money must be a commodity. Since money must be a commodity, two important conclusions follow: (1) the exchange value of every commodity in terms of the money commodity is determinant (given the value of the latter), and (2) that the circulation of the money commodity derives from the circulation of all other commodities. Increases in the availability of the money commodity result in money lying in dormant hoards, awaiting its call to serve when production increases. Representations of money create a "veil" over this process, affecting only the rate at which these representations exchange (or symbolize) commodity money. It is an illusion that variations in the circulation of valueless money stimulate or reduce the circulation of commodities. Empirically, this illusion arises from the fact that the state tends to increase the availability of valueless money in periods of rapid accumulation, so it appears that valueless money circulates commodities, though such an increase is not necessary, a point we pursue in the next chapter. If one accepts this illusion at face value, the circulation of valueless money and its impact upon nominal prices appears as the proof of the essentially conventional nature of money, rather than what it is, the assertion of the primary role of commodity money. If the analysis begins with valueless money, it is discovered that nominal prices depend upon its quantity; then one can argue backwards to commodity money and conclude erroneously that the supply of commodity money would also determine prices.[31] By beginning with a form or symbol of money that serves only as a medium of circulation, it becomes possible to attribute this sol-

---

[31] "The erroneous opinion that it is . . . prices that are determined by the quantity of the circulating medium, and that the latter depends on the quantity of the precious metals in a country; this opinion was based by those who first held it, on the absurd hypothesis that commodities are without a price, and money without a value, when they first enter into circulation." *A Contribution*, p. 125.

itary function to money itself. So, by a circuitous route, pre-suming money has but one function makes it possible to conclude that no other functions exist, and money as a stand-ard of value, store of value, and means of payment are con-veniently written out of the theory.

The intrinsic role of commodity money in capitalist soci-ety is not merely a theoretical issue, but is recognized by bourgeois writers, however inaccurately. From the end of World War II to the early 1960s, the international capitalist economy enjoyed a period of relative stability and more or less continuous expansion. As we shall see, in periods of ac-cumulation the role of money as means of circulation is dominant, and the other functions recede in importance. In such periods, like the postwar boom, it appears that the money commodity becomes demonetized, largely irrelevant. In this context, the bourgeoisie of the major capitalist coun-tries worked through institutions such as the International Monetary Fund to endorse the latent role of gold and to re-place it with monetary symbols.

With the end of the postwar prosperity, however, the ef-forts to abandon gold as a means of international payment became increasingly unsuccessful.[32] Indeed, the frenzied speculation in gold during the late 1970s reflected the inade-quacy of national currencies as a store of value. The role of money as a store of value is perhaps nowhere more impor-tant than in international transactions. In the mid-1970s, for-eign exchange reserves of all capitalist countries were in the area of $160 billion, and the countries' real claims on com-modities were continuously threatened by exchange rate de-preciation, particularly of the dollar (the major form of re-serve holdings).[33] In this context, bourgeois publications as

---

[32] Writing of international finance in 1975, Morris says, "One conclusion springs at once from this analysis. SDRs [Special Drawing Rights] are the worst possible form of international reserves. They have all the disadvan-tages of dollars and gold and none of their advantages." Jacob Morris, "The Weird World of International Money," *Monthly Review* 27 (November 1975), p. 12.

[33] *Ibid.*

respectable as *The Times* of London and *Fortune* carried articles seriously considering a return to the gold standard.[34] A
detailed analysis of the international financial crisis of the
1970s is beyond the scope of this book. However, such an
analysis would reveal the glittering commodity basis of
money, which asserts itself in periods of economic crisis.

[34] *The Times* (London), February 1, 1980; and *Fortune*, April 7, 1980, "The
New Allure of the Gold Standard."

CHAPTER V

CREDIT, CREDIT CRISES, AND SOCIAL CAPITAL

A. The "Capital Relation"

In capitalist society, the role of commodity money is hidden not only by representations of money (paper notes and token coins) but also by credit, which can be defined as contractual indebtedness. Credit, in effect, allows for circulation without money, so that the exchange of commodities coincides with the accumulation of indebtedness. When these debts fall due and are not or cannot be further extended, money serves as a means of payment. Thus with the development of credit transactions, money falls out of use as a means of circulation and becomes the medium for canceling debts; i.e., the payment for transactions that have already occurred. In this case, money does not circulate, but lies idle alongside indebtedness as "the independent form of existence of exchange value."[1] The analysis of credit involves the relationship between commodity circulation independent of money, and the assertion of the role of commodity money when debts must be canceled. In short, we must consider the contradiction arising from the fact that different functions of money give rise to different forms of monetary equivalency.[2]

Money in capitalist society is the medium by which labor power and the means of production are set into motion. This

[1] "Insofar as actual payments have to be made, money does not serve as a circulating medium, but as the individual incarnation of social labor, as the independent form of existence of exchange value, as the universal commodity." *Capital*, I, p. 137.

[2] "This contradiction comes to a head in those phases of individual and commercial crises which are known as monetary crises." *Ibid.*, p. 137.

role of money does not occur spontaneously but is the consequence of particular social relations. Money in the abstract or money in itself is not a claim upon the productive forces of society unless labor has been separated from the means of production and both, therefore, exist as commodities. The function of money as capital presupposes the capital relation itself. The capital relation is the presence of free wage labor (dispossessed and alienated labor), and the existence of free wage labor allows money to function as a command upon the labor power of individuals.[3] The conversion of money into capital, the marshaling of the productive forces through exchange, represents particular class relations and the operation of a particular form of class society, capitalism.

A characteristic of this class society is that its reproduction requires the circulation of commodities and, alongside them, money. Since capitalist society is the first society in which the circulation of commodities and money is general, it appears that circulation is the dominant moment or process in capitalist society. This unique feature of capitalism is the basis of erroneous theories that seek to explain the operations of the system in terms of circulation. The most extreme example is neoclassical economic theory, which takes the conditions of production as given, and analyzes only the circulation of commodities. When circulation rather than relations of production is treated as primary, it is a small step to attribute an active role to money. This is ahistorical, for money has existed in varying degrees of development in many societies without giving rise to capitalist accumulation.

Given the development of capitalist social relations, the accumulation of capital appears as the accumulation of money. The circuit of capital, M-C ... P ... C'-M', begins and ends with money, so that its point of departure and culmination seem to be the expansion of money. As a conse-

---

[3] "The capital relation during the process of production arises only because it is inherent in the act of circulation, in the different fundamental economic conditions in which buyer and seller confront each other, in their class relation. It is not money which by its nature creates this wealth; it is rather the existence of this relation which permits of the transformation of a mere money-function into a capital-function." *Capital*, II, p. 32.

quence, it appears that the expansion of capital is not material, but the mere generation of money. From the point of view of capitalists, this irrational aspect of accumulation—money-more money—assumes a real existence. In fact, for some capitalists, it is possible merely to convert money into more money without going through the process of production. This is the case of money capital or finance capital, in which capital in money form, capital as finance, becomes a commodity. As finance, capital is not productive, but must be converted into commodities in order to set production in motion and produce surplus value. The analysis of credit is the investigation of the development of money capital as a form of wealth accumulation independent of, and in some cases, dominant over, industrial capital.

B. Hoarding and Money Capital

In the previous chapter we showed that capitalist society generates hoarding of money because of the nature of money itself. Since the money commodity need not be realized, it naturally comes to rest in hoards when it is not all required for circulation. In hoards it remains capital and in this way differs from hoarding in precapitalist society.[4] Hoarded money is unproductive, but from the point of view of the capitalist class, it is capital nonetheless, and as such commands a rate of return. The basis for the return is fictitious capital, symbols of contractual ownership and indebtedness—stocks, bonds, treasury bills, and so on. Capital in this form is fictitious in that it is a mere representation of a generalized claim on surplus value, rather than a direct claim of ownership on any material object. In consequence, the market value of these paper assets may be only loosely related to the market value of the means of production they nominally

---

[4] "But it must be borne in mind that hoarding takes place in the simple circulation of commodities long before this is based on capitalist production. The quantity of money existing in society is always greater than the part of it in actual circulation. . . . We find [in capitalism] here again the same hoards, and the same formation of hoards, but now as an element immanent in the capitalist process of production." *Ibid.*, p. 497.

stand for. The markets for financial assets in a capitalist society represent the mechanism by which idle money asserts itself as potential capital. Bourgeois analysis reverses the relationship. In bourgeois theory, the buying and selling of fictitious capital is viewed as the mechanism by which capital performs an active role, in that these financial transactions are viewed as determining the movement of capital. While, as we shall see, these transactions do affect the distribution of finance among capitalists, their existence arises from the necessity that money be idle, hoarded. The central point can be summarized as follows: in bourgeois theory, money is held in the form of financial assets only because it receives a return to induce capitalists to do so; in reality, the existence of hoarding is independent of the motivation of individual capitalists, and it is the existence of hoarded money that, under capitalist relations, calls forth a "return" to hoards. This return represents a portion of surplus value, arising in production. The role of hoards vis-à-vis fixed capital is treated in Chapter VII.

A moment of historical reflection makes clear that under capitalism it is hoarding that demands a return for itself, not the return that stimulates hoarding. During precapitalist times wealth was accumulated in hoards, frequently in the form of a general equivalent, i.e., money. However, except for those specifically involved in the usury trade, accumulated wealth did not "earn" a return.[5] It did not do so because of the limited function of money in society. When neither labor power nor the means of production are commodities, money is not a potential claim upon the surplus labor of society, but merely exchangeable for a limited set of the products of labor. Money in this case cannot enter into the process by which wealth is increased, since this is done within nonmonetized social relations (serfdom, guild system, etc.). Since money in such societies plays a restricted role in wealth expansion, it can lay no claim to a return—*it is not capital*. It serves as part of the process of the distribution

---

[5] See Marx's discussion of usury, *Capital*, III, XXXVI.

of products and this only to a limited extent.[6] For this reason, precapitalist interest-bearing money exists to facilitate luxury consumption and state expenditure (e.g., hiring of mercenaries), as it cannot enter into the productive sphere to any great degree.[7]

To consider the nature of credit, we must first explicitly introduce interest-bearing capital into the circuit of capital, which is done by adding an additional step or moment to M-C-M',

$$M^*\text{-}M\text{-}C \ldots P \ldots C'\text{-}M' \; (= M + m, \; m = SV).^8$$

In the first step, money capitalists lend money to industrial capitalists (M^*-M). The first M is designated by a star to indicate that while $M^* = M$, the transaction requires that the money capitalists receive back money in excess of the amount M. Before considering how this excess is determined, it is necessary to explain why the moment M^*-M occurs. Its function is not obvious, since no value is created by it. This is also true of M-C and C'-M', but both of these nonetheless are necessary steps in the circuit of capital. The first, M-C, is the way in which alienated labor is reunited with the means of production, the only way this can occur in a society of free wage labor.[9] The moment C'-M' effects the realization of value (and surplus value), the conversion of commodities in particular into the general equivalent, so that their abstract quality, value, is manifest in its most general form. This provides the basis for the re-initiation of the circuit. The circuit M-$C \ldots P \ldots C'M'$ encompasses the process of the production of surplus value, and in this proc-

[6] See Chapter II, above, where the development of commodity circulation is discussed.

[7] We are ignoring merchant's capital and the precapitalist development of fictitious capital. This in any case was relevant to a very limited portion of hoarded wealth and is part of an analysis of the historical role of merchant's capital. *Capital*, III, Chapter XX.

[8] M denotes money, C, the commodities labor power and the means of production, C' the newly produced commodities, and P the amount of production. The dots reflect the fact that capital is momentarily out of circulation. SV stands for surplus value, so $M' - M = m = SV$.

[9] Marx analyzes the moment M-C in detail in *Capital*, II, Chapter I.

ess capital must assume different forms—money capital, productive capital, commodity capital (M, C, C'). For capital as a whole, the step $M\star$-M seems redundant, for value is neither created nor is its form altered. We appear to have merely a change of the hands that hold the money-capital, a change that is neither quantitative nor qualitative.

The step cannot be explained by arguing that $M\star$-M is necessary in order to provide the finance for the expansion of production. The level of operation of capital as a whole in any period is set by the material production of the previous period. More specifically, the surplus product of one period sets the limit to accumulation in the next, since only what has been produced can subsequently be employed as means of production and means of subsistence for the working class. If the step C'-M' (realization) is assumed to occur smoothly, then the money necessary for the conversion of money capital into productive capital is also assumed.[10] This is another way of demonstrating the passive role of money.[11]

In fact, the step $M\star$-M cannot be accounted for or understood at the level of capital as a whole, but arises from the interaction of many capitals, reflecting the process of centralization (the redistribution of capital). At the level of capital as a whole, we can treat accumulation as being the result of the capitalizing of realized surplus value, but this cannot hold for many capitals, since it would render impossible all but the most trivial quantitative and qualitative aspects of

---

[10] In fact, for capital as a whole, M-C and C'-M' are the same step. The sale of the means of production is the realization moment for some capitals and simultaneously the conversion of money capital into productive capital for others. For the means of subsistence the process is more complex, since they are directly bought by workers.

[11] "Whereas the surplus product, directly produced and appropriated by the capitalists . . . is the real basis of the accumulation of capital . . . although it does not actually function in this capacity until it reaches the hands of [industrial capitalists], it is on the contrary absolutely unproductive in its chrysalis state of money—as a hoard and virtual money capital in process of gradual formation—runs parallel the process of production in this form, but lies outside of it. It is a dead weight of capitalist production." *Capital*, II, p. 502.

accumulation.[12] The process of accumulation involves the quantitative alteration of the social division of labor, as some industries expand and others contract, and the introduction of technical change, in which the more efficient capitals expand at the expense of the less efficient either in the same branch of industry or by leaping into another. Both of these processes would be virtually impossible if capitalists were limited in their accumulation to the surplus value realized in the moment $C'-M'$. Accumulation requires, in Marx's phrase, that money capital be "wholly detached from the parent stock."[13] The development of a class of money capitalists effects this detachment.

At the level of capital as a whole, the system of credit and fictitious capital exists as a consequence of hoarding. At the level of many capitals, it provides the mechanism by which capital can be redistributed in order to bring about changes in the structure of production and technology. What is being redistributed are claims upon the surplus product of society, surplus value. In order that some capitals expand beyond the limit set by the surplus value they realize as profit, surplus value must become detached from its source. This detachment mechanism involves the development of what Marx called "social capital."[14]

C. Credit, Interest, and Social Capital

In order that surplus value be redistributed from some capitals to others to facilitate centralization, it is necessary that

[12] It would treat accumulation as expanded reproduction. On this distinction, see John Weeks, "The Process of Accumulation and the 'Profit Squeeze' Hypothesis," *Science and Society*, 43 (Fall 1979).

[13] "With the absolute increase of the value of the annually reproduced virtual money-capital its segmentation also becomes easier, so that it is more rapidly invested in any particular business, either in the hands of the same capitalist or in those of others. . . . By segmentation of money capital is meant here that it is wholly detached from the parent stock in order to be invested as new money capital in a new and independent business." *Capital*, II, p. 502.

[14] *Capital*, III, Chapter XXVII.

ownership be detached from the units of production. Just as the development of capitalism initially requires the abolition of individual private property in favor of capitalist private property,[15] the maturing of capitalism requires the abolition of individualized private property among capitalists in favor of the socialization of ownership to capital as a whole. Increasingly capitalists no longer own factories or hold any direct claim upon the material means of production, but through ownership of fictitious capital hold a claim on a portion of total surplus value wherever and in whatever form produced. In Marx's words, "The capital . . . is here directly endowed with the form of *social capital* . . . as distinct from private capital, and its undertakings assume the form of social undertakings as distinct from private undertakings. It is the abolition of capital as private property within the framework of capitalist production itself." [Emphasis added.][16]

What is abolished is the industrial capitalist's ownership of the means of production. This ownership is passed to the money capitalist, thereby "transforming the actual functioning capitalist into a mere manager."[17] Before exploring the consequences of this change, we note that the discovery of "managerial capitalism" by bourgeois economists in the 1930s[18] was anticipated by Marx over half a century before. The illusions created by the development of socialized capitalist ownership provide the elements of the "managerial revolution" analysis, and these are treated below. This analysis discovered that the industrial capitalist as a property owner, having personified the capital-relation in the youth of bourgeois society, later becomes an obstacle to capitalist development, as much of an anachronism in his ownership role as the feudal lord or guildmaster and a historical curiosity.

The separation of the ownership of capital from the con-

---

[15] This distinction was discussed in Chapter II.
[16] *Capital*, III, p. 436.
[17] *Capital*, III, p. 436.
[18] A. A. Berle and Gardner Means, *The Modern Corporation and Private Property* (New York: Macmillan, 1932).

trol of the production process is not a sociological phenomenon but the result of the need to centralize capital in the process of accumulation. This centralization is achieved through the development of credit and the formal ascendency of financial capital over industrial capital. This ascendency may take the form of the control of industry by banking interests, as Lenin discussed in *Imperialism*.[19] The ascendency of financial capital is not, however, a question of the role of institutions but of the nature of mature capitalism. Whatever institutional form social capital assumes, finance capital remains dominant in the sense that the claim on surplus value becomes detached from the level of the production unit. It is in this sense that the epoch of imperialism is the period in which financial capital dominates industrial capital.[20] This domination is established by the nature of accumulation, not by the relationship between institutions.

In summary, with the development of credit, the ownership of capital becomes the ownership of surplus-value-producing capital in the abstract, not the ownership of specific use-value-producing means of production. The concept of capital as a whole moves from the category of ideas to an actual social category, as capitalists own capital in general, in its most abstract form, fictitious capital. These contractual documents represent claims on social labor, though the expansion of value is determined in the material process of production. Private property as such recedes, and all ownership is ownership of a claim on surplus value.[21]

The manner by which this is accomplished is through the credit system, in which capital itself becomes a commodity. Indeed, we can define capitalist credit as the commodity

---

[19] V. I. Lenin, *Imperialism, the Highest Stage of Capitalism*, in *Collected Works* (Moscow: Progress Publishers, 1974), Vol. XXII.

[20] *Ibid.*

[21] "With the development of social production the means of production cease to be means of private production and products of private production, and can thereafter be only means of production in the hands of associated producers. . . . However, this expropriation appears within the capitalist system in a contradictory form, as appropriation of social property by a few." *Capital*, III, p. 440.

form of capital; it is the existence form of the commodity "capital." At the outset, it is difficult to grasp the idea of capital being a commodity, for we are not referring to labor power and the means of production, which this capital can exchange for, but to capital itself, as *finance*.

As pointed out, the step M^*-M involves no expansion (production) of value, nor any change in the form of capital. Actually, no exchange in the normal sense occurs, since the recipient of the finance gives up no commodity or money in the step, but promises to return the loan quantitatively augmented at a future date. Thus, the commodity capital, to the extent it is circulated by an exchange, exchanges against itself. Every commodity has a use value and an exchange value. In the case of the commodity capital, the use value is that it can function as capital, be exchanged against productive commodities, whose consumption creates surplus value. Thus its use value arises from the existence of the capital-relation, which allows money or finance in credit form to be a claim upon the average profit of society.[22] The concept of use value applies here but in a unique way. In the case of all other commodities, use value is the result of their natural, material properties. When these commodities are used productively in the labor process, their use value is consumed either at once or over time, depending upon whether they are circulating or fixed capital.[23] How they are consumed differs from labor process to labor process, and to a certain extent owing to the customs of society, but they are in any case consumed materially—"their substance disappears."[24]

The use value of the commodity capital, in contrast, has no basis in the material form of this commodity, since capital

[22] "The use value of the loaned capital lies in its being able to serve as capital and, as such, to produce the average profit under average conditions." *Capital*, III, p. 352.

[23] The distinction between circulating capital (capital advanced for labor power and intermediate commodities) and fixed capital (capital advanced for machinery, buildings, etc.) is treated in Chapter VII.

[24] "In the case of other commodities the use-value is ultimately consumed. . . . In contrast, the commodity capital is peculiar in that its value and use value not only remain intact but also increase, through consumption of it." *Capital*, III, p. 352.

is a purely social relation. That is, capital is not money, nor commodities, nor the means of production as such, since all of these can and do exist without being capital. Money spent by the working class is not capital, for it is not advanced for labor power or the means of production. Commodities need not be capital if they are not produced under capitalist relations, i.e., peasant production in underdeveloped countries. And machinery and tools existed long before the capitalist epoch. Thus, capital is a social relation in which each of these, money, commodities, means of production, serves momentarily as the form this social relation assumes in its life cycle. In consequence, the use value of capital as a commodity is *purely* social, completely dependent upon the prior existence of commodity production (in the sense defined in Chapter II). Capital has no material form as such, though it may be represented in material form. As money capital, it could be in the form of gold (a money commodity); as productive capital it exists as a claim on human effort and purchased means of production; and as commodity capital it is freshly produced commodities awaiting realization as money capital again. But none of these material forms represents the use value of capital. Their use values are material characteristics of the commodities independently of their function as capital. As capital, their consumption occurs in a certain context, for a certain purpose—the production of surplus value. A tree may yield fruit that is eaten. If the tree grows in an orchard of a capitalist farm, and the fruit is sold, it is not capital that yields fruit, it is still the tree that generates fruit. The failure to make this distinction between the material aspect of production and the social relations under which production is organized gives rise to the bourgeois concept of capital as a factor of production. The neo-Keynesian critique of this treatment of capital is derived precisely from this distinction, though the implications of the critique are not pursued to any degree.[25]

Capital itself is not consumed but moves through the

[25] See G. Harcourt, *Some Cambridge Controversies in the Theory of Capital* (Cambridge, England: Cambridge University Press, 1972).

process of commodity production and circulation in tact, as the socialized, abstract representation of commodities. As a commodity, it must have a price, and this definitional and practical necessity presents a paradox, since loaned capital *is* price; the commodity form of capital presents itself as a certain amount of money, or representation of money. In the case of all other commodities, price is the money form of the commodity. However, for capital, the commodity exists as money, implying the apparently absurd contradiction that capital has a price, prior to being a commodity. In the circulation of capital as a commodity, a price form need be created for that which already is price.

The interest form provides the solution to this quandary and is, by its nature, irrational.[26] It is irrational in that we have a price (money form) that cannot be expressed in monetary units. This reflects, first, that what is involved is a redistribution of surplus value, not its production. Second, and related, the capital commodity is the only commodity that cannot exchange at its value, for if it did, this would imply a zero price. Loan capital represents a certain amount of social labor or value and enters the production process when it is converted into commodities, whose use value is consumed in the labor process. The price of loan capital—capital as a commodity—reflects the expansion of value that occurs after the $M^{\star}$-M step. It is a deduction from surplus value produced in the labor process, so that the rate of interest requires the quantitative division of surplus value into interest and profit of enterprise. As with all commodities, the market price of the capital commodity is determined by supply and demand. However, with all other commodities, the fluctuations in supply and demand occur around the value of a commodity, so that market price has a determinant "center of gravity" (socially necessary abstract labor time). Competi-

---

[26] "Interest, signifying the price of capital, is from the outset quite an irrational expression. The commodity in question has a double value, first a value, and then a price different from its value, while price represents the expression of value in money." *Capital*, III, p. 354.

tion brings about the general rate of profit in all branches of industry as a tendency.

Since the capital commodity has no value but represents value, there is no center of gravity around which the market interest rate fluctuates. There are no laws determining the rate of interest other than competition itself. The capital commodity is not produced, but exists because of the division of the capitalist class into two functional groups. If by some magical stroke the class of money capitalists were swept away, there would be no interest category.[27] This would be impossible, however, since it would prevent the social appropriation of surplus value by capital as a whole (social capital), which in turn would block the necessary redivision of surplus value that brings about shifts in the division of labor. Just as profit and the rate of profit are capitalist categories that lose any relevance under socialism, so the interest form disappears with the passing of capitalist society.

As we have seen, the interest form is a necessary development in the capitalist mode of production. While interest reflects no contribution of money capital to the production of value, it is essential to the process of the centralization of capital. This division of surplus value between interest and industrial profit ("profit of enterprise" Marx called it) is essentially different from the division of new value into surplus value and the value of labor power. If we consider the product of living labor as a mere quantity of value, then it appears that we have a threefold division—wages, profit, and interest—reflecting the claims of three groups—proletarians, industrial capitalists, and money capitalists. But this division should not be viewed quantitatively in the first instance. The division between surplus value and the value of labor power arises from the qualitatively different position of two classes.

[27] "It is indeed only the separation of capitalists into money-capitalists and industrial capitalists that transforms a portion of the profit into interest, that generally creates the category of interest; and it is only the competition between these two kinds of capitalists which creates the rate of interest. . . . If all capital were in the hands of the industrial capitalists there would be no such thing as interest and rate of interest." *Capital*, III, pp. 370, 379.

The proletariat, separated from the means of production, surrenders its control over the labor process and, in doing so, cedes to capital the entire product. The proportion of new value that reaches the proletariat as wages is determined by the value of labor power. Without this qualitative differentiation between workers and capitalists, no surplus value is possible. A class division, derived from the relations of production, generates a quantitative division of value. Further, this quantitative division is theoretically determinant, since it is based upon a commodity with a determinant value, labor power.[28]

The division between interest and profit of enterprise is secondary, in that it requires (or presupposes) the prior division of value into surplus value and the value of labor power. In the case of interest and profit of enterprise, the division is purely quantitative, in that it does not follow from a class division as such. Industrial capitalists and money capitalists are both part of the class that holds monopoly over the means of production. Their relation to the means of production is essentially the same; they are partners in the process of capitalist exploitation, having established a division of labor among themselves in order to facilitate accumulation. The division of surplus value between them is the result of their intraclass competition and takes the form of fluctuations in the price of a valueless commodity, loan capital.[29]

[28] For a discussion of the value of labor power, see Weeks, "The Process of Accumulation."

[29] "If we inquire further as to why the limits of a mean rate of interest cannot be deduced from general laws, we find the answer lies simply in the nature of interest. It is merely a part of the average profit. The same capital appears in two roles—as loanable capital in the lender's hands and as industrial, or commercial, capital in the hands of the functioning capitalist. But it functions just once, and produces profit just once. In the production process itself the nature of capital as loanable capital plays no role. . . . Two entirely different elements—labor power and capital—act as determinants in the division between surplus value and wages . . . these are functions of two independent variables, which limit one another; and it is their *qualitative difference* that is the source of the *quantitative division* of the produced value. . . . Nothing of the kind occurs in the case of interest. Here the qualitative differentiation . . . proceeds rather from the purely *quantitative division* of the same sum of surplus value." *Capital*, III, p. 364.

While the struggle between capital and labor obviously affects the share of interest and profit of enterprise insofar as that struggle has an impact upon total surplus value, the net product should not be analyzed in terms of a threefold division (or fourfold, if we include rent). The division between the value of labor power and surplus value is determined in production, while the division between profit of enterprise and interest is determined purely in circulation. In the former case, exchange (between capital and labor) reflects a division prior to that exchange, while in the latter case it is the exchange itself which affects the division. That is, in the first case, exchange is only a part of a value-determining process that involves the interaction of production and circulation. The material process of production is the basis for the value of the commodities that workers consume, and these commodities and their values establish the value of labor power. In addition, total net value is determined in part at the point of production by the class struggle over the intensity and duration of work. Thus, the exchange between capital and labor is merely the final moment in a process of material production and class struggle. In the latter case, the exchange between industrial capitalists and money capitalists, exchange is a determining factor in its own right, since the commodity exchanged, capital, has not been produced.

The nature of the interest form and the moment it arises in the circuit of capital generates the illusion that the rate of interest determines the rate of profit, while in actuality the reverse is true. In Chapter III we developed the concept of the average rate of profit, which is the ratio of surplus value to capital advanced, for capital as a whole. This rate of profit is the basis of the general rate of profit received in each industry. However, because surplus value undergoes this quantitative division we have been considering, the general rate of profit cannot be observed directly; it has no empirical form.[30] What one observes is a rate of interest and a rate of industrial or commercial profit. Further, the interest form

[30] "The general rate of profit, however, appears only as the lower limit of profit, not as an empirical, directly visible form of the actual rate of profit." *Ibid.*, p. 367.

appears as the reward for owning capital, thus the return to capital itself. The money capitalist, by lending to the industrial capitalist, obtains the formal ownership of the working capital employed in the production process. Money capitalists represent capital as ownership, while the industrial capitalists represent the functioning of capital.[31] To the industrial capitalist, it appears that profit is a residual, purely derivative from the interest rate, since a higher interest rate implies a lower profit of enterprise, and the rate of interest confronts the industrial capitalist as a contractual obligation prior to production. Thus the profit received by the industrial capitalist seems not to be the result of owning capital (since this has shifted formally to the money capitalist), but from his own skill and enterprise in organizing production.[32]

If one takes the twofold division of surplus value as given, it then is possible to argue that the distribution of new value reflects a difference in productive contributions: the worker supplies labor power and receives a wage; the entrepreneur supplies organizing ability and receives profit, and the money capitalist provides capital and receives interest. This is the view of neoclassical theory, in which each of these—labor, entrepreneurial ability, and capital—are treated symmetrically as material inputs to production.

As we have seen, the basis of this illusion is the quantitative division of surplus value, rendered necessary by the accumulation process, which requires the redistribution of surplus value among capitals. The twofold division of surplus value in no way reflects any productive division of labor or

[31] "Interest-bearing capital is capital as *property* as distinct from capital as a *function.*" *Ibid.*, p. 379.

[32] "In relation to [the industrial capitalist] interest appears therefore as the mere fruit of owning capital, of capital as such abstracted from the reproduction process of capital . . . while profit of enterprise appears to him as the exclusive fruit of the functions which he performs with the capital . . . a performance which appears to him as his own activity. . . . This qualitative distinction is by no means merely a subjective notion of the money-capitalist, on the one hand, and the industrial capitalist, on the other. It rests upon an objective fact, for interest flows to the money-capitalist . . . who is the mere owner of capital." *Ibid.*, p. 378.

productive functioning in general. The division reflects the separation of the ownership of capital from the function of capital, the separation of surplus value from its origin for the purpose of converting it into capital for expanded production.

D. CREDIT CRISES

The division of surplus value derives from the development of credit, and the development of credit necessarily generates credit crises. The analysis of the role of credit in capitalist accumulation requires a brief review of the function of money as a means of payment. The extension of credit facilitates exchanges without payment. A credit transaction is an exchange in which the borrower receives commodities with a promise to make payment in the future. This may be direct, as when one industrial capitalist provides another with short-term credit in a particular sale. Such credits in Marx's time were called "bills of exchange," though we shall use the term "suppliers' credits." Alternatively, one industrial capitalist may borrow from a money capitalist in order to purchase commodities from a second industrial capitalist. While the two types of credit transactions can have different implications in the accumulation process, they both have the characteristic that the commodity exchange creates a debt, and commodities circulate as a consequence of growing indebtedness, not as a result of the parallel circulation of money. In these exchanges, money is not a medium of circulation, but a means of payment for previous transactions. Obviously, if credit is defined as money, such a distinction cannot be made, and the function of money as a means of payment becomes identical with the function as means of circulation. The central insight of Marx's theory of money in mature capitalist society is the distinction between money and credit, which implies the distinction between money as means of payment and means of circulation. These distinctions provide an understanding of why, when the circuit of capital is interrupted, "the whole crisis seems to be merely a credit and money crisis."[33]

Let us assume that the process of accumulation is proceeding normally, in that the average rate of profit is stable or rising and surplus value is converted into productive capital, so that the mass of commodities and their value increase in each circuit of capital. This accumulation is brought about by the successive advancing of more capital, and the demand for the means of production—a demand among capitalists—progressively expands. As we have seen, the centralization of capital requires that these intracapitalist exchanges be on the basis of credit. As the accumulation process continues, exchange becomes increasingly independent of money, and a pyramid of credit-indebtedness builds up. In this expansionary process, the predominant form of credit may be among industrial capitalists, and there need be no limit to the expansion of such credit, except the accumulation process itself, which sets the material limit to the mass of the means of production that can circulate.[34]

In this expansionary period, the monetary demand by industrial capitalists is for the means of circulation. This limited role can be satisfied by a mere symbol of future payment, either through borrowing from money capitalists or by mutual agreement between producers. In this period, industrial capital achieves a semi-independence of money capital, for if money capitalists, for whatever reason, decline to supply sufficient credit, industrial capitalists can meet their demands among themselves. In prosperity there is no reason money capitalists should so decline, since what Marx called "the regularity of returns" on industrial capital insures the interest return. However, this semi-independence asserts it-

---

[33] *Ibid.*, p. 490.

[34] "Just as these mutual advances of producers and merchants make up the real foundation of credit, so does the instrument of their circulation, the bill of exchange, form the basis of credit-money paper. . . . These do not rest upon the circulation of money, be it metallic or government-issued paper money." *Ibid.*, pp. 400-401.

self by keeping the rate of interest low, since promissory notes between industrial capitalists are an adequate substitute for bank-capital.

The key characteristic of this prosperity period is that the dominant monetary function is means of circulation, so the demand for money as such declines with the rapid accumulation of indebtedness. Since monetary demand is here the demand for means of circulation, and this can be satisfied by any acceptable representation of money (actually, representation of future payment), it appears that anything can serve as money. The prosperity period endorses the illusion that money need have no value; and as a medium of circulation it need not. This primacy of the function of means of circulation reflects the eagerness of industrial capitalists to expand production, convert surplus value into productive capital, so they need only a monetary form to bridge the gap between commodity capital and productive capital.[35] As this continues, there is nothing to prevent the development of indebtedness (credit) in excess of the amount of commodity money that could potentially circulate. The credit system facilitates the expansion of production to its material limit,[36] unrestrained by any dependence upon money as such.

When the expansion comes to an end, the dominant monetary function changes, and money as such asserts itself as a means of payment. In a subsequent chapter we consider why accumulation should be interrupted. Here we assume that the regularity of returns comes to an end and less capital is advanced in each successive circuit of capital. At this moment, the demand among capitalists declines, the volume of exchanges declines, and previously contracted purchases fall due for payment. Suddenly, industrial capitalists require an adequate monetary form as means of payment; money as-

[35] That is, to achieve realization of the newly produced commodities, then the purchase of the means of production and labor power.

[36] Here we do not refer to the exhaustion of the reserve army (though this is a possibility), but the limit set by the supply of the means of production.

serts itself, and with it money capital, capital as ownership.[37] The shift in monetary demand from means of purchase to means of payment occurs for all industrial capitalists at the same time. The credit system they developed among themselves during prosperity was based upon a presumption of continued expansion, and once that expansion ends, this pyramid of credit becomes a demand for payment that must be satisfied.

In the prosperity period, capital as function is dominant, capital as self-expanding value. In this period the social relations of production facilitate the production of surplus value, and the forces of production are stretched to their limit. When this expansion comes to an end and the production-exchange-production cycle is interrupted, capital as ownership asserts itself. This contradiction between the material process of production and the social relations that make that production viable under capitalism manifests itself in a conflict between industrial and money capital that threatens a credit collapse and forces a credit crisis.

The point needs to be developed further, since it provides the key to understanding why a credit crisis has apparently irrational consequences. Capitalism at its essence is a form of socialized production, and production is a material process. The purpose of this production from the standpoint of capital is the production of surplus value. The production of surplus value is not sufficient for the reproduction of the capital relation; it must also be distributed in a manner that allows for that reproduction. The circuit of capital involves both of these processes, production and circulation. The production process involves capital as function, the domination of labor in order to achieve exploitation. The distribution of surplus value involves ownership, the institutional claims

---

[37] "In times of stringency, the demand for loan capital is a demand for means of payment and nothing else; it is by no means a demand for money as a means of purchase. At the same time, the rate of interest may rise very high, regardless whether real capital, i.e., productive and commodity capital, exists in abundance or is scarce. The demand for means of payment is mere demand for convertibility into *money*." *Capital*, III, p. 515.

upon surplus value already produced. The credit system separates these two, and the separation is personified in the industrial capitalist and the money capitalist.[38]

As long as the production of surplus value proceeds uninterrupted, the industrial capitalist achieves a certain independence of the money capitalist, which reflects the dominance of the material (production) over the social (distribution). However, once the production of surplus value is no longer adequate, capital as a whole enters a period when losses must be distributed as well as gains. In this period the rivalry among capitalists asserts itself, as a struggle begins to determine who within the class will be survivors. This struggle manifests itself as industrial capitalists are forced to liquidate their debts; i.e., convert credit to money. Money capitalists are then the arbitrators of the struggle for survival. The availability of credit drastically declines and industrial capital lies idle. The sudden demand for money as means of payment threatens the value of fictitious capital, and thus the structure of ownership.

During prosperity, a volume of credit develops that bears no fixed relation to the available money to cancel those debts. Unless there is some drastic adjustment mechanism, a part of the accumulated debt cannot be paid off and will be found valueless.[39] This drastic mechanism is the devaluation of commodities.[40] As the expansion of capital ends, com-

[38] "[W]e must proceed from the assumption that the money capitalist and the industrial capitalist really confront one another not just as legally different persons, but as persons playing entirely different roles in the reproduction process. . . . The one merely loans [capital], the other employs it productively." *Ibid.*, p. 372.

[39] "In a system of production, where the entire continuity of the reproduction process rests upon credit, a crisis must obviously occur—a tremendous rush for means of payment—when credit suddenly ceases and only cash payments have validity. At first glance, therefore, the whole crisis seems to be merely a credit and money crisis." *Ibid.*, p. 490.

[40] "In times of a squeeze, when credit contracts or ceases entirely, money suddenly stands as the only means of payment and true existence of value in absolute opposition to all other commodities. Hence the universal depreciation of commodities, the difficulty or even impossibility of transforming them into money, i.e., their own purely fantastic form. Secondly, credit-

modities go unsold, and their market prices fall, which implies a rise in the value of money. This rise in the value of money protects the market value of fictitious capital and claims on indebtedness. The money necessary, but quantitatively insufficient, to redeem the accumulated debts inflates in exchange value. When the value of private credit is threatened, the capitalist mode of production itself provides a partial solution to this problem. The insufficiency of money for conversion of credit is accompanied by the destruction in the market of the values of commodities, so that a credit crisis causes the concrete use values to be sacrificed for the abstract—credit. In this manner, the ownership of capital is protected at the expense of the functioning of capital.[41] In this process of canceling debts, the increase in the exchange value of money need not result from an attempt by all creditors to have their loans paid in gold, a point we develop below. A credit crisis occurs because the form of money adequate for facilitating exchange is not satisfactory for canceling debts. What was an adequate form of equivalency among capitalists during the expansionary period proves not to be a general equivalent when debts must be canceled.

We can now summarize the process that necessarily generates credit crises in capitalist society. The accumulation of capital requires changes in the division of labor that are brought about by the movement of capital. Were it the case that individual capitals could expand only on the basis of the surplus value they each realize as profit, the ability of the

---

money itself is only money to the extent that it absolutely takes the place of actual money to the amount of its nominal value. With a drain on gold its convertibility, i.e., its identity with actual gold, becomes problematic. Hence coercive measures, raising the rate of interest, etc., for the purpose of safeguarding the condition of this convertibility." *Ibid.*, p. 517.

[41] "This basis [of convertibility] is given with the basis of the mode of production itself. A depreciation of credit-money . . . would unsettle all existing relations. Therefore, the value of commodities is sacrificed for the purpose of safeguarding the fantastic and independent existence of this value in money. . . . In former modes of production, this does not occur because, on the narrow basis upon which they stand, neither credit nor credit-money can develop greatly." *Ibid.*, p. 517.

system as a whole to alter the division of labor would be severely limited. The redistribution of surplus value for accumulation is achieved through the credit system, which involves a differentiation between the control of the production process and the claim upon surplus value (capital as function and capital as ownership). As accumulation proceeds, a structure of debt develops, which is not quantitatively limited by the available commodity money. When expansion comes to an end, the accumulated debt must be paid off in all or large part. At this moment, the demand for capital as a commodity is a demand for means of payment. Money capitalists seek to redeem debts in a form insolated from changes in value, and industrial capitalists seek to do the same with their produced commodities. The sudden rush for money as means of payment pushes up the rate of interest, which further reduces profit of enterprise. Commodities go unsold, some debts cannot be paid off or only paid off in part, and the market value of fictitious capital is depreciated. Finally, we must stress that the credit crisis merely reflects a problem in the production of surplus value, a problem we have presupposed, to be explained later. But given this presupposition, a credit crisis is the necessary outcome of the accumulation process.

E. Socialized Credit and Inflation

The course of a credit crisis described above involves a depreciation of commodity prices, so that the interruption of the circuit of capital is accompanied by deflation. In the last twenty years in capitalist countries, recessions have increasingly been associated with rising prices, and our theory of money and credit should be able to account for this if it is to claim generality.

Recently Fine has developed an explanation of the coincidence of inflation and the interruption of the circuit of capital (recession),[42] and the following analysis draws upon his

[42] Ben Fine, *Economic Theory and Ideology* (London: Edward Arnold, 1980).

work. All discussion of credit must be made in terms of particular institutional forms, since credit is a creation of the institutional division of the functioning and ownership of capital. These institutional forms change as capitalism develops and matures. In the previous section, we assumed that credit was private, in the form of suppliers' credits (between industrial capitalists) or loan capital (from money capitalists to industrial capitalists). There has been no reference to the state, so implicitly it was assumed that the expansion of private credit was not accompanied by any expansion of representations of money by the state, in whatever form.

As argued in Section C, the process of accumulation transforms private capital into social capital so that surplus value realized as profit may be redistributed from some capitals to others to facilitate a redivision of labor. This provides the basis for credit crises and stimulates action by the capitalist class, through the state, to control these crises. This state interference reflects the monopolization of sectors of the economy by certain capitals,[43] which we consider in the next chapter.

We argued that a credit crisis develops because of a sudden increase in the demand for money for means of payment, when the quantity of credit has outgrown the quantity of commodity money available for its cancellation. This quantitative imbalance can be rectified in form by the state's increasing the supply of representations of money. Achievement of this can be direct, by the issuance of more paper currency, or indirect, by the state's increasing its own indebtedness, i.e., through the purchase by the state of its bonds from capitalists. In either case, the effect is to socialize credit. In this situation, all bankruptcies and business failures are not prevented, but a general shortage of the means of

---

[43] "[Social capital] is the abolition of the capitalist mode of production within the capitalist mode of production and hence a self-dissolving contradiction, which *prima facie* represents a mere phase of transition to a new form of production. It manifests itself as such a contradiction in its effects. It establishes a monopoly in certain spheres and thereby requires state interference." *Ibid.*, p. 438.

payment is prevented. Representations of money circulate to replace private debt. This may involve merely a change in form of state indebtedness, if the state circulates more representations of money by exchanging them for its own securities held by private capital. Such open market operations would reduce the tendency of the rate of interest to rise by increasing the prices of state bonds, a process laboriously analyzed in bourgeois theory.

By referring to the theory developed in Chapter IV, we can see that such socialization of credit does not resolve the basic problem created by the growth of private credit, but merely changes the form of its manifestation. The state in effect has created a situation in which all the representations of money cannot be converted into the money commodity. Attempts by capitalists to convert representations of money created by the state into a store of value results in the depreciation of those representations. What appeared in our earlier discussion as a threat to the market value of private debt now appears as a general decline in the exchange value of paper money. The state may attempt to guarantee convertibility, in which case there will be a rush to commodity money, exhausting state and private hoards of commodity money (or threatening to do so). If convertibility into the generally equivalent money commodity is suspended, capitalists will seek to exchange their intrinsically worthless representations of money for commodities that are near-substitutes for the money commodity, or to other national currencies, when we introduce the complication of the division of capitalist society into countries. Precisely this process occurred in the 1970s, when there was a run on precious metals and certain national currencies such as the Deutsche Mark.

What appeared in an earlier stage of capitalist development as a collapse of commodity prices and stock and bond prices now breaks out as an inflationary spiral accompanied by speculation in commodities. This process, which has characterized the developed capitalist countries since the mid-1960s demonstrates the necessary role played by commodity money in the circulation of capital. The circuit of capital is incomplete until commodities are realized in their "fantastic form" as money. Credit buying does not achieve this realization, but postpones it. When the expansion of capital comes to an end, the motive to accumulate is replaced by the motive to hoard, to store value for future accumulation. The state's economic policies cannot prevent this; they can only alter the form that hoarding takes, and alter the manifestations that result from the rush to hoard by capitalists. Therefore, it should come as no surprise that some bourgeois writers should call for a return to the gold standard as a means of guaranteeing the worth of representations of money.

CHAPTER VI

THE COMPETITION AMONG CAPITALS

A. INTRODUCTION

In previous chapters we have stressed that capitalist society is unique in that its reproduction requires the circulation of the products of labor in the form of commodities. This circulation, integrated with the production of use values (characteristic of all societies), rests on the basis of isolated production. The circulation of commodities, along with the parallel circulation of money, is the mechanism by which isolated producers are integrated into a system of social reproduction. Competition, a concept we have alluded to repeatedly, is the interaction of isolated, independent producers. This concept is of central importance to the understanding of capitalist society. We have, in fact, prepared the ground for an analysis of competition, and it remains only to develop the analysis.

Marx's methodological break with bourgeois political economy was so sharp and complete as to constitute a methodological revolution. This break derives from the insight that capitalism is a historically unique mode of social reproduction. Most Marxian writers formally recognize this methodological break, but elements of bourgeois analysis and method continue to find currency in Marxian writings, particularly in the treatment of competition. In general, it seems to be the view, among Marxists and non-Marxists alike, that while Marx broke new ground in other areas, his treatment of competition was the same as that of bourgeois theorists. This presumption manifests itself in the view that Marx's theory as outlined in *Capital* is historically specific to competitive capitalism, and must be amended in light of capitalism in its monopoly stage.

These concepts of competitive and monopoly capitalism are closely related to the Marxist debate over the theory of imperialism. It is beyond the scope of this book to treat that debate in any detail, but the concepts of competition, monopoly, and imperialism are so intertwined (and often confused) in the literature that some reference cannot be avoided. Most modern Marxist writers proceed on the presupposition that contemporary capitalist society is noncompetitive.[1] Those who hold this view frequently cite Lenin as a supporting authority, for in various writings he describes capitalism of his time in terms that superficially seem to imply that competition among capitals was no longer a significant force.[2] The overall view of the monopoly capital school is that, in the present stage of capitalist development, competition has been virtually eliminated, and this has fundamentally altered the nature of capitalist society. The most important change, in this view, is that capitalist society is no longer prone to crises, but to long-term stagnation.

This general analysis is in clear contrast to that made by Marx, who demonstrated that it is the dynamism of capitalism that gives rise to its contradictory tendencies (a point pursued in Chapters VII and VIII). Specifically, accumulation brings the contradictions of capitalism to a head. It is first under capitalism that the development of the forces of production is inherent in the process of production. This, in part, is what makes capitalism a *progressive* form of the social organization of production compared to previous modes of production. The development of the forces of production is not the result of the desires of individual capitalists, but the result of the internal contradictions of this mode of produc-

---

[1] The work of Baran and Sweezy is well known, but they are far from alone in arguing that under imperialism "competition" has been eliminated. See, for example, Samir Amin, *Unequal Development* (New York: Monthly Review Press, 1976), pp. 102ff.

[2] V. I. Lenin, *Imperialism, the Highest Stage of Capitalism*, in *Collected Works* (Moscow: Progress Publishers, 1974), XXII; and "Imperialism and the Split in Socialism," *Collected Works*, XXIII.

tion. The most basic internal contradiction is that capitalist production is formally isolated, and private labor must be converted into social labor, so that under capitalism products become commodities, combining in one object use value and exchange value. The necessary condition for the existence of the capital relation is that labor power be a commodity, as we have seen. Further, the existence of labor power as a commodity creates the conditions for and necessity of competition. That is, competition does not derive from the existence of many capitals ("companies"), but from the capital relation itself. In turn, competition thrusts upon capitalists the necessity to cheapen commodities. The development of the productive forces must be undertaken by capitalists in order to survive in the competitive struggle. This necessity affects all capitalists and all capitals, no matter how large or powerful.

By its nature, the interaction of capitals forces each capital to reduce the labor time embodied in commodities, which raises the productivity of labor. This process of increasing the number of commodities each worker produces per unit of time Marx called the "expelling" of living labor, a process we consider in detail in the next two chapters. As we shall see, this dynamic process of technical change ("revolutionizing of the means of production") is the source of contradictory tendencies that give rise to the undermining of the accumulation process. It is the development of the forces of production that undermines capitalism. Marx was unambiguously clear that he believed that the dynamism of capitalism creates the necessity of crisis. Referring to the tendency of the rate of profit to fall, the manifestation of the basic contradictions of capitalist reproduction, Marx wrote

> The progressive tendency of the general rate of profit to fall is, therefore, just *an expression peculiar to the capitalist mode of production* of the progressive development of the social productivity of labor.

> The means—unconditional development of the productive forces of society—come continually into conflict with the limited purpose, the self-expansion of the ex-

isting capital. The capitalist mode of production is, for this reason, a historical means of developing the material forces of production . . . and is, at the same time a continual conflict between this its historical task and its own corresponding relations of production.[3]

But the development of the productive forces does not occur automatically; it is the consequence of the antagonistic and contradictory interaction of many capitals. The argument over the presence or absence of competition and technical change in contemporary capitalist society is, therefore, an argument over the basic nature of capitalism.[4]

B. THE PLACE OF COMPETITION IN MARX'S THEORY

Baran and Sweezy have written that "the Marxian analysis of capitalism still rests in the final analysis on the assumption of a competitive economy."[5] This statement implies a certain method on Marx's part; namely, that competition has a par-

[3] *Capital*, III, pp. 213, 250.

[4] And the debate is not new. It was one of the many issues that divided "The Opposition" (Trotsky and his supporters) from the majority of the CPSU (Bolsheviks). In 1926, Stalin wrote: "That Trotsky objects to Lenin's theoretical thesis concerning the law of uneven development is not at all surprising, for it is well known that this law refutes Trotsky's theory of permanent revolution . . .

"What is it that accentuates the unevenness and lends *decisive* significance to the uneven development in the conditions of imperialism? . . .

". . . that the colossal and *hitherto unparalleled* development of technique, in the broad meaning of the word, makes it easier for certain imperialist groups to overtake and outstrip others in the struggle for markets, for seizing sources of raw materials, etc.

"And it could not be otherwise . . . only in the period of developed imperialism did the colossal technical possibilities show themselves." J. Stalin, *Works*, VIII, 1926 (Moscow: Foreign Languages Publishing House, 1954, reprinted London: Red Star Press, Ltd., n.d.), pp. 326, 329.

[5] P. A. Baran and P. M. Sweezy, *Monopoly Capital* (New York: Monthly Review Press, 1966), p. 4. They go on to say, "[Marx] never attempted to investigate what would at the time have been a hypothetical system characterized by the prevalence of large-scale enterprise and monopoly" (pp. 4-5).

ticular status in his analysis, the status of an externally imposed assumption. From this it follows that his conclusions must be sensitive to making alternative assumptions; and, further, that the choice among assumptions about competition is an empirical one. Baran and Sweezy have attributed to Marx the methodology of bourgeois economic theory, where competition has such a status of an assumption. In fact, Marx constructed his theory of competition in a completely different manner from the method of bourgeois theory.

To show this, we first should explain the bourgeois view of competition, which defines competition as the free and unregulated interaction of individuals in pursuit of their interests in the act of exchange. Having defined competition in this way, the bourgeois theorists can then enumerate the conditions necessary for competition to prevail: many buyers and sellers, free entry and exit from the market, etc. For them, competition is a question of numbers and the size of competitors; as a consequence, it is a trivial issue of how many sellers or how many buyers exist for a particular commodity. If there are "a lot," we have competition; if there are "a few," we have "restricted," "limited," or "monopolistic" competition. And if, unfortunately, there is only one seller (buyer), we have "monopoly" ("monopsony"). One might call this "the quantity theory of competition."

This treatment of competition is characteristic of the method of bourgeois political economy in general, in that competition is considered ahistorically and as a relationship purely in exchange.[6] The treatment is ahistorical in that it applies equally to all modes of production where exchange is present; i.e., the conditions for competition could apply to a slave economy as well as one based on wage labor. Presup-

---

[6] This is also true of the neo-Ricardian theory of competition, which is essentially no different from the so-called neoclassical treatment. The neo-Ricardian approach is not considered separately here for that reason. For a very clear discussion comparing the neo-Ricardian method to Marx's method, see Ben Fine and Laurence Harris, "Controversial Issues in Marxist Economic Theory," *Socialist Register* (1976), pp. 141-178.

posed are the social conditions that allow for competition. Divorced from any specific discussion of capitalism, this theory is confined to the act of exchange, a social relation characteristic of modes of production other than capitalism (see Chapters I and II). The bourgeois theory is not wrong in the sense of wrongly describing a real phenomenon. The phenomenon to which it addresses itself (the struggle among capitals for market shares) is a real process, a process generally recognized by Marxists and non-Marxists alike. Further, it is correct to place the act of exchange in a central place in the process of competition. What is incorrect, as we see below, is the treatment of exchange divorced from the class relations that are unique to capitalism. Marx's treatment of competition is not an alternative to the bourgeois approach, but a treatment that begins in an entirely different manner and encompasses the manifestation of competition in the exchange of commodities as a part of a general theory of competition.

In bourgeois theory, competition among capitals is introduced as an external force, and in the absence of this external force none of the general economic laws of bourgeois economics holds: production and consumption are no longer efficient, the laws of distribution are suspended, and supply and demand cannot be used as an analytical tool in the short run or long run. This is because bourgeois theory is grounded in the sphere of circulation—exchange—and within this sphere no phenomenon can be considered without reference to competition. For this reason, competition among capitals in bourgeois theory appears not only as the vehicle by which economic laws manifest themselves but also as the origin and cause of these laws. The implications of this last point can be seen fully only after we consider Marx's theory of competition. Indeed, it could be argued that competition is the central theoretical element in bourgeois theory, from which all of its generalizations derive.

In value theory, accumulation is the key element, the process that gives rise to all the important generalizations regard-

ing capitalist reproduction.[7] Although accumulation and
competition are closely related, the former can be conceptualized and understood prior to an analysis of competition.
This is because accumulation is the progressive expansion of
the circuit of capital, and the circuit of capital is first analyzed
for capital-as-a-whole, without reference to the interaction
of many capitals. Here we must stress that we refer to the
competition among capitals, for since the basis of capital is
the separation of labor from the means of production, the
circuit of capital cannot involve an abstraction from the competition between capital and labor, i.e., the class struggle itself.

The circuit of capital is the circuit of self-expansion of
value, M-C-M', and the basis of this self-expansion (given
the historical conditions for capital's existence, free wage labor) is the production of surplus value. The production of
surplus value requires the concepts of constant and variable
capital, and the use of these concepts allows a distinction
between the production of absolute and relative surplus
value. These latter concepts are not ideal constructions, but
correspond to real processes, the speed-up and the lengthening of the working day (absolute surplus value) and the
progressive application of machinery to the labor process,
which increases the division of labor (relative surplus value).
As capitalism develops, the production of relative surplus
value becomes the primary way of increasing surplus value
and gives rise to what Marx called "the general law of capitalist accumulation," which is the endogenous generation of
surplus labor power—the industrial reserve army. All of this
analysis brings one through Volume I of *Capital*, and it is
not necessary in the analysis to deal with the competition
among capitals. Indeed, to do so would obscure the analysis
by introducing a complex concept—"competition among
capitals"—prior to an explanation of the simpler concepts
upon which it is predicated. One cannot consider the way

[7] In what follows, I am indebted to discussions with Ben Fine and draw
on points raised in Ben Fine and Laurence Harris, *Re-reading Capital*, Chap.
1.

individual capitals interact in the accumulation process until the possibility of accumulation is explained, which itself is understood through developing the concept of capital-as-a-whole. It is possible to advance so far in the analysis of capitalism while abstracting from competition because the accumulation process is essentially a production process carried out under specific relations of production, and these specific relations of production require analysis of the exchange between capital and labor, but not the exchange between capitals. However, the competition among capitals is subsumed within this analysis and is not subsequently developed independently.

Once we consider the realization process and the distribution of surplus value among capitals and among its phenomenal forms—rent, interest, profit of enterprise—the competition among capitals presents itself for analysis and must be conceptualized. We have considered one aspect of this competition, that between money capital and industrial capital. It became necessary to do so in order to account for the process by which qualitative changes are brought about during the accumulation process. Prior to considering this particular aspect of competition it was not necessary to make any assumptions about it, since the issue did not present itself as long as we dealt with capital-as-a-whole. It cannot be stressed too much that while bourgeois theory initiates its analysis of capitalism by postulating competition or non-competition among capitals and cannot proceed even a single logical step without doing so, value theory develops the theory of accumulation without needing to refer to the mutual interaction of capitals.[8] As a final point, competition among capitals could be considered when establishing the basis of accumulation, in that the analytical elements of the concept are present in the concept of capital itself, but to do so would

[8] To take just one example, the tendency of the rate of profit to fall is clearly set out in Volume I of *Capital*, as are the counteracting tendencies, though not identified as such because Marx has not presented the concept of the rate of profit, which derives from the integration of production and exchange (the task of Volume II).

complicate the analysis without advancing it. For this reason Marx sums up the role of the competition among capitals as follows: "Competition merely *expresses* as real, posits as an external necessity, that which lies within the nature of capital; competition is nothing more than the way in which the many capitals force the inherent determinants of capital upon one another and upon themselves. Hence, not a single category of bourgeois economy, not even the most basic, e.g., the determination of value, becomes real through free competition alone."[9]

In other words, competition is the mechanism by which the underlying laws of accumulation manifest themselves. Specifically, one can point to the law of value, which we have considered in detail. Competition does not generate or even make possible the operation of this law, for its basis is free wage labor and the means of production circulating as commodities. Competition merely allows for the expression of the law. Another way to put it is that the fundamental concept here is that of the relations of production (free wage labor), and these create the possibility of both the law of value and the competition among capitals at the same conceptual level.

At points in his writings, Marx states that competition is the mechanism by which the essence of capitalist social relations is transformed into their appearance. We have considered an example of this. While the basis of capitalist accumulation is the appropriation of unpaid labor, the wage form masks this exploitation in the guise of an equal exchange. Workers compete among themselves over wages and capitalists compete with workers. A second example of the distorting effect of competition is in the price form. As we have shown, the competition among capitals brings about a deviation of price from value, which gives the illusion that dead labor creates value. These two examples can be multiplied, which led Marx to observe that in competition every

[9] *Grundrisse*, p. 651.

relationship is reversed.[10] From this distorting character of
competition, we can conclude that it is an analytical mistake
to begin one's theory with an analysis of competition, for
this would be to begin at the level of distorted appearances.
Rather, one should begin at the level of social relations and
ask why there should be competition.

C. COMPETITION AS THE "INNER NATURE OF CAPITAL"

When Marx defines competition, he does so in terms of capital-as-a-whole, writing that "conceptually, *competition* is
nothing other than the *inner nature of capital*, its essential character, appearing in and realized as the reciprocal interaction
of many capitals."[11] As we shall see, this seizes upon the
social relationship of the buying and selling of labor power
as the basis of the competition among capitals. In order to
understand Marx, we must see that the bourgeois theory of
competition, although ahistorical in method of analysis, is in
fact merely an idealized description of the particular historical character of capitalist production. Unlike utopian socialists such as Proudhon, Marx did not believe that there had
once existed, or could ever exist, a society of free producers,
each small and independent, each pursuing his or her interests. Whereas socialists such as Sismondi and Proudhon
looked back to a pre-monopolistic competitive era, Marx
scorned such ideas as illusion.[12] Marx argued that such a
view of capitalism—and of competition—was merely an ideological fantasy, a description of the historical conditions
that freed capital from feudal barriers to its self-expansion,
presented as natural law.

Prior to the epoch of capitalism, economic life was regu-

---

[10] ". . . [in competition] all determinants appear in a position which is the
inverse of their position in capital in general. There price determined by
labor, here labor determined by price, etc., etc." *Grundrisse*, p. 657.

[11] *Ibid.*, p. 414, second emphasis added.

[12] Later, Lenin also analyzed these utopian socialist views, defending
Marx's method. See V. I. Lenin, "A Characterization of Economic Roman-
ticism," in *Collected Works* (Moscow: Progress Publishers, 1974), II.

lated in a particular way within a particular mode of production. These regulations involved guild membership, state trading monopolies, and many other mercantile trappings. With the emergence of capitalism as the dominant mode of production, economic life was also regulated, but by capital for capital. The intellectual spokesmen of the rising bourgeoisie, such as Adam Smith, described the latter regulations as "free competition," giving an ideological justification to the new order.[13] In the broadest sense, both systems are characterized by monopoly—one the monopoly of the landlord class, the other the monopoly of the capitalist class. What Smith did not do, and his successors down to Samuelson have not done, was to analyze the conflict among capitals.[14] This Marx took as his task. To suggest, as Sweezy and Baran do, that competition is the existence of many competitors, and the absence of monopolized and centralized production, is to use bourgeois ideology as theory. For example, there were a large number of manors in feudal society, but no competition. Numbers are not the key, nor is the size of competitors; the key is the social relations that determine and regulate the interaction of producers.

The bourgeois definition and treatment of competition are ahistorical, for competition is treated without first explaining why there should be competitors. This is the same mistake as initiating an analysis of value without explaining why there are commodities, discussed in Chapter II. In both cases the general production of products as commodities is presup-

[13] Henryk Grossmann, "Marx, Classical Political Economy and the Problem of Dynamics, Part I," *Capital and Class*, 2 (Summer 1977).

[14] Marx is at his most insightful on this: "Because competition appears as the dissolution of compulsory guild membership, government regulation, internal tariffs and the like within a country . . . in short, as the negation of the limits and barriers peculiar to the stages of production proceeding capital . . . , it has [therefore] never been examined even for this merely negative side, this, its merely historical side, and this had led at the same time to the even greater absurdity of regarding it as the collision of unfettered individuals who are determined only by their own interests . . . and hence as the absolute mode of existence of free individuality in the sphere of consumption and of exchange. *Nothing can be more mistaken.*" *Grundrisse*, p. 649.

posed. Put another way, bourgeois theory initiates the discussion of competition at a relatively low level of abstraction and, as a result, treats it in extremely complex form, at a level where one must at the outset account for price competition, product differentiation, capital movements, barriers to those movements, and the process of centralization. As a consequence, the analysis proceeds eclectically, and the forms the competitive struggle take under capitalism do not derive from the concept itself, but appear as exceptions to it. It is to avoid this eclecticism that we define competition simply as "the inner nature of capital itself," and with this simple concept we can move to more complex concepts such as competition among capitals and, more complex still, concepts such as "price competition."

Capital as a social relation represents the integration of production and exchange in a reproductive circuit. Competition among capitals arises in this integration. As Fine and Harris write, "in reality competition between capitals is predicated upon the circuit of capital-in-general . . . for without the relations between *capital and labor* encompassed by these simple circuits competition *between capitals* cannot exist."[15] For this reason, the basis of competition is the buying and selling of labor power. Every phenomenon of capitalism need not be traced back to first principles, but concepts must be constructed at the point where the phenomenon to be analyzed can no longer be abstracted from.

Competition is the inner nature of capital in that it arises from the contradiction between the process of production and the process of circulation, which are united in industrial capital ("capital as such," as Marx put it). While capital unites production and circulation, it does so in a contradictory way, through the medium of free wage labor. Because labor power is a commodity, the product of capitalist production must be exchanged. The reproduction of capitalist society necessitates that the use values arising from production be realized as money. It is first under capitalist society that the

---

[15] Fine and Harris, *Re-reading Capital*, p. 1:4.

surplus labor of direct producers cannot be appropriated generally in material or natural form, but must be converted
into money.[16] The first and most basic form of competition
is the competition between capital and labor, not for the distribution of the value produced, but over the organization of
production itself. This competition is a class struggle over
the most basic aspect of any society—the control of production. And the subsumption of labor to capital[17] is the basis
for the competition among capitals.

Capital exists by virtue of the presence of free wage labor,
on the one hand,[18] and the monopolization of the means of
production by a class, on the other. The existence of free
wage labor facilitates not only the exploitation of labor but
the exploitation of labor in the service of capital and its de-
ployment at the will of capital; i.e., where it will bring forth
the largest profit. The feudal ruling class exploited labor, but
because labor was united with the means of production, this
exploitation was of an essentially immobile labor force. Free
wage labor liberates the exploiting class to exploit labor under different circumstances.[19] We have used the term "free"
wage labor repeatedly, and now its full implications come
clear. Prior to capitalist society, labor was "unfree" in that
its mobility was narrowly limited within servile social relations—New World slavery being perhaps the most extreme
type of such limitations. When such social relations were destroyed in favor of free wage labor, workers become free in
the narrow sense of not being permanently tied to particular
exploiters. What received the potential for unconditional
freedom and liberation as a result of the demise of servile
relations was capital, not labor.

[16] Robert Brenner, "The Origins of Capitalist Development: A Critique
of Neo-Smithian Marxism," *New Left Review*, 104 (July-August 1977), pp.
3-12.

[17] In the Appendix to the Penguin edition of Volume I Marx analyzes this
process. Karl Marx, *Capital* (London: Penguin, 1976).

[18] Thus, *capital* is the negation of feudal monopoly. I consider the significance of this below.

[19] Marx writes: "It is not individuals who are set free by free competition;
it is, rather, capital which is set free." *Grundrisse*, p. 650.

The inner nature of capital is the capital-labor relation, for it is this social relation, involving the exchange of capital against labor power, that brings the production process under the domination and direct control of capital. This inner nature of capital is based upon free wage labor, and begins with an exchange, an exchange which is prior to production and prior to the circulation and realization of commodities. It is that purchase of labor power by capital that creates the conditions for competition. The necessary conditions for bourgeois production—free wage labor and a market for the means of production—mean that the possibility of capital marshaling the forces of production for an invasion of branches of industry where the rate of profit is above average is always present. Thus competition under capitalism is not determined by conditions in what bourgeois economists call the "product market," but determined by the existence of a market for labor power. While a capital can momentarily monopolize the sale of a particular commodity, a capital cannot monopolize the market for labor power (or "monopsonize"). In part this is because of the reserve army, which is continuously generated by capital. But the existence of the reserve army itself is the consequence of labor power's being a commodity, and this is the basis of competition among capitals. There is a more fundamental point, which the existence of a reserve army of the unemployed reflects. In capitalist society, because labor is separated from the means of production, their unification for the purpose of carrying out production is of a particular type.

Free wage labor involves the permanent separation of labor from the means of production in terms of ownership and control, and necessitates the repeated uniting of labor with the means of production by capitals through each circuit of capital via the buying and selling of labor power. Since the unity of labor and the means of production is a moment in the circulation of capital and always incomplete quantitatively (the existence of the reserve army), each capital's control over labor power is momentarily and quantitatively incomplete. The unification is also incomplete in that capitalists buy not workers themselves but their capacity for work. Once the period for which labor power has been contracted passes, the link between a particular group of workers and a particular capitalist is broken. Thus we have a contradiction: while capital as a whole asserts its monopoly over labor as capitalism develops (by the tendency to eliminate all sources of livelihood except wage labor), this monopoly takes the form of the competition among capitals. It is in this sense that "free competition is the relation of capital to itself as another capital."[20] Under capitalism, the relations of production—labor power as a commodity—prevent the permanent monopolization of production in any branch of industry, for the form of capital's exploitation of labor continuously creates the conditions for competition.

At this level of conceptualization, competition among capitals is only an inherent tendency. The form this competition assumes cannot be analyzed without considering particular stages of capitalist development, a point pursued in the following section. Competition, as it appears, is determined by the sophistication of the credit system, the role of the state, and the development of the productive forces.[21] The basis of competition can be analyzed, as we have done, through abstracting from the complexities of reality, but competition as it manifests itself incorporates all those complexities.

It is important to break with the idea that competition is the struggle over sales of particular commodities, which is the conclusion of bourgeois analysis. This is certainly an aspect of competition, but an aspect that presupposes the buying and selling of labor power. The exchange of commodities (that is, circulation of products for the purpose of realizing their exchange value) predated the development of

[20] Commenting on the view by Smith that competition is the absence of extra-economic restraints to pursuit of self-interest, Marx writes: "But competition is very far from having only this historical significance, or merely being *this negative* force. Free competition is the relation of capital to itself as another capital, i.e., the real conduct of capital as capital." *Ibid.*, p. 650.

[21] J. A. Clifton, "Competition and the Evolution of the Capitalist Mode of Production," *Cambridge Journal of Economics* (June 1977).

capitalism. It was a characteristic of merchant's capital, which Marx called the form of capital $(M\text{-}C\text{-}M')$ without the essence of capital.[22] Control over the market for a single commodity or a number of commodities by one or several capitals temporarily suppresses the manifestation of competition in a particular market, but does not eliminate or even reduce competition among capitals. Control over a market does not touch the source of competition, which is the existence of free wage labor. To eliminate competition, it would be necessary to eliminate labor power as a commodity, as was the case under feudalism.

Since a market for labor power is the necessary condition for capital, to assume competition is to assume capitalism; the existence of capitalism implies competition. Capitalism involves the movement of capital; competition is this movement.[23] We can now understand why bourgeois economists must assume or posit competition at the outset of their analysis. Competition is the "inner nature" of capital, its force manifested in all the complex appearances that capital's movement assumes, and none of these appearances can be considered independently of competition, though the underlying basis of capitalist reproduction can be.

To this point, the competition among capitals has been analyzed without treating centralization and concentration. Centralization (redistribution of existing capital) does not reduce competition—causality runs the other way, from competition to centralization. Competition gives rise to capitalist monopolies, but such monopolies are not the antithesis of competition; i.e., monopolies are not the negation of competition.[24] On the contrary,

---

[22] *Capital*, III, p. 326.

[23] Marx takes Ricardo to task, "Ricardo presuppose[d] the absolute predominance of free competition in order to be able to study and to formulate the adequate laws of capital. . . . What Ricardo has thereby admitted, despite himself, is the *historic nature* of capital, and the limited character of free competition, which is first the free movement of capital and nothing else." *Grundrisse*, p. 651.

[24] Proudhon, anticipating Baran and Sweezy, wrote, "*Monopoly* is the inevitable doom of competition, which engenders it by continual negation of

We all know that competition was engendered by feudal monopoly. Thus competition was originally the opposite of monopoly and *not monopoly the opposite of competition*. So that *modern* monopoly is not a simple antithesis, it is on the contrary *the true synthesis*.

Thesis: Feudal monopoly, before competition.

Antithesis: Competition.

Synthesis: Modern monopoly, which is the negation of feudal monopoly as it implies the system of competition, and the negation of competition insofar as it is monopoly.[25]

The contradictions inherent in the social relation capital generate centralization, but this does not result in the elimination of the competitive contradiction. Competition is the negation of feudalism and not a function of the number of competitors. Competition arose as a consequence of the elimination of the material basis for feudal monopolies. That material basis was the immobility of laborers, the appropriation of surplus product in natural form ("in kind"), and the union of labor with the means of labor. Capitalism arose through the separation of labor from the land (and the means of labor in general), which created the conditions for the appropriation of surplus product in the form of surplus value. Since the process of centralization does not eliminate the alienation of labor (in the Marxian sense described in the previous sentence), but intensifies and advances it, centralization does not eliminate competition. Modern monopoly emerges as the synthesis of the competitive contradiction and the process of centralization. Capitalist monopoly is thus "the unity of opposites." The monopolies that stalk the pages of the writings of Baran and Sweezy have no existence beyond the work of those authors. For these monopolies, which at will set prices, control and suppress innovation, and the like,

itself. . . . Monopoly is the natural opposite of competition." Quoted by Marx in *The Poverty of Philosophy*, Karl Marx and Frederick Engels, *Collected Works* (New York: International Publishers, 1976), VI, p. 194.

[25] *Ibid.*

are idealistic resurrections of "feudal monopoly, before competition."

The buying and selling of labor power does not establish
the forms that competition will assume or its intensity.
These two aspects of competition require an analysis of
credit and accumulation. As we argued in the previous chapter, credit is the mechanism that brings competition about.
Competition among capitals can be seen in essence as the
attempt to redistribute (centralize) capital, and the credit
mechanism is the lever for this redistribution. Since the
credit system develops and becomes more sophisticated as
capitalism develops, competition among capitals is facilitated
as capitalism matures. The process of accumulation, on the
other hand, sets the context of the competitive struggle,
whether it occurs within a contracting or expanding circuit
of reproduction of social capital.

D. Competition in the Era of Advanced Capitalism

The necessity of competition comes out of capital itself and
is established as a characteristic of capitalism prior to any
discussion of many capitals. Indeed, the existence of many
capitals is the consequence of competition; Marxian theory
turns the bourgeois analysis of competition on its head. Since
competition arises from the inner nature of capital, "capital
exists and can only exist as many capitals, and its self determination therefore appears as their reciprocal interaction
with one another."[26] Thus, the form the capital relation necessarily takes is that of many capitals, and capitalism without
competition is a contradiction in terms. This theoretical conclusion has been subject of intense debate among Marxists
and socialists since the turn of the century. V. I. Lenin and
Karl Kautsky, one the leader of the world's first socialist
state, the other the leader of the reformist social democrats
of his day, waged polemical arguments over precisely this
issue. Kautsky argued that capitalist development tended to-

[26] *Grundrisse*, p. 414.

ward a "single world trust" in a world of "ultra-imperialism" and, in such conditions, competition would be eliminated. By implication, this meant for Kautsky that intercapitalist wars, generated by competition for markets, would also be eliminated. Lenin sharply attacked this view on the grounds that competition and conflict intensified as capitalism developed.[27] The theoretical analysis of competition is also relevant to the present debate over the nature of Soviet society.[28] Although this latter issue is beyond the scope of our discussion, we note that if the Soviet Union is capitalist, as some contend, then it is characterized necessarily by capitalist competition.

The Marxian analysis of competition reverses another aspect of bourgeois analysis. As noted, bourgeois theorists look back to a "golden age" of competition, when competitors were many, production units small, and competition was free. This follows logically from the quantity theory of competition. This view is totally ahistorical. Competition, since it derives from the inner nature of capital, develops and intensifies as capital develops. When competitors were small and many, competition was primitive and embryonic. It is with the development of capital in its most advanced form, monopoly capital, that competition, too, develops to its fullest extent.[29] It is possible to be more concrete. In the early development of capitalism (1750-1850 in England, for example), competition was under-developed in that there remained precapitalist fetters on the expansion of capital. Further, the incomplete development of financial institutions made it difficult for capitalists to obtain sufficient money capital to invade other branches of industry. In this early phase of capitalism, competition took the primitive form of

---

[27] Lenin, "Imperialism and the Split in Socialism," and *Imperialism*.

[28] It follows from Marx's analysis of competition that the competitive contradiction cannot be suppressed under capitalist relations of production, no matter what the institutional form of property ownership. On this issue and the question of the Soviet Union, see C. Bettelheim, *Economic Calculation and Forms of Property*.

[29] *Grundrisse*, p. 651.

the struggle among capitals within a single branch of industry. When capitalism as the dominant mode of production is fully developed, however, the development of credit institutions advances, and capitalist competition reaches a higher stage, wherein competition manifests itself in the flow of capital between branches of industry, which themselves may be monopolized.

> In practical life we find not only competition, monopoly, and the antagonism between them, but also the synthesis of the two, which is not a formula, but a movement. Monopoly produces competition, competition produces monopoly. Monopolists compete among themselves; competitors become monopolists . . . and the more the mass of the proletarians grows as against the monopolists of one nation, the more desperate competition becomes between monopolists of different nations. *The synthesis is such that monopoly can only maintain itself by continually entering into the struggle of competition.*[30]

In the age of monopoly capitalism, capitalist competition has burst through the confines of one branch of industry, burst through the confines of one country, and rages on an international scale. With this theoretical background, one can, for example, understand Lenin's writings on imperialism. When Lenin comes to define imperialism, as opposed to characterizing or describing it, his definition is disarmingly simple, "If it were necessary to give the briefest possible definition of imperialism we should have to say that imperialism is the monopoly stage of capitalism."[31] This is the stage of capitalism in which competition rages on a worldwide scale. Closely related to the process of competition among capitals as Marx developed it is the law of uneven development, considered in detail in the next two chapters. Uneven development describes the tendency under

---

[30] Marx and Engels, *Collected Works*, VI, p. 197. Those who think Marx "could not anticipate" the era of imperialism and monopoly capitalism might reflect on this passage from *The Poverty of Philosophy*.
[31] V. I. Lenin, *Imperialism*, p. 266.

capitalism for the forces of production to develop un-
evenly—between capitals in the same branch of industry, between branches of industry, between regions and countries.
What is fundamental is the uneven development of capital,
and this may take many forms.

As we pointed out at the beginning of this chapter, one of
the most important aspects of competition is its impetus to
the development of the productive forces in capitalist society. Marx argued, and we shall argue in the next two chapters, that technical change generates crises in capitalist societies. Since the contradiction that forces development of the
productive forces upon capital is competition, the theory of
crises derives in part from the analysis of competition. We
have argued that competition is internal to social capital as a
whole; the existence of competition cannot be assumed, nor
is it in the first instance an empirical question. It is a fundamental internal contradiction of capital as a social relation.
With this understood, it becomes clear that competition develops and intensifies as capitalism develops; i.e., with the
fuller development and maturing of capital, all the contradictions of this mode of production develop and intensify. This
analysis is in contrast to bourgeois theory, which is either
idealistic (invoking competition by assumption) or empiri-
cist. What it ignores is capital as a social relation, looking at
the form of (number of capitals) rather than the essence of
things.

F. Competition and the Movement of Capital

To this point we have primarily considered the basis of the
competition among capitals, identifying that basis as the
buying and selling of labor power. The form competition
takes is the movement of capital, which is the process by
which the average rate of profit is converted into a general
rate of profit. To review briefly these concepts, the average
rate of profit is the rate of profit for capital-as-a-whole, and
the general rate of profit is that average generalized to each

industry.[32] In light of the discussion of competition, we can now further consider this process of the formation of the general rate of profit.

Previously, we demonstrated that the rate of surplus value exists as a social aggregate, independently of any particular industry. This follows from the social nature of the value of labor power, so that it is incorrect to conceive of the rate of surplus value varying across industries and the aggregate to be a mere weighted average of rates in different industries. For any particular capital, the rate of profit is the ratio of surplus value realized as profit to capital advanced. This rate of profit for a capitalist enterprise presupposes the interaction of capitals (competition). To demonstrate this, let us consider a particular capital, whose price calculation can be written as follows

$$P_1 = (1 + \pi)(a_{ij}p_i + wL).$$

Where P_1 = price of commodity 1;
  π = actual rate of profit earned;
  a_{ij} = the physical amounts of the
      means of production used up
      in the labor process;
  p_i = unit price of the means of production
  w = the money wage; and
  L = the quantity of living
      labor employed.

If the value of labor power is given, the profit earned by a particular capital depends upon the prices paid for the means of production (the p_i's) and the efficiency of use of the means of production and labor power (the a_{ij}'s and L). Prices are determined by the movement of capital. If we begin artificially with the situation where exchange values are equal to values, this implies unequal rates of profit across industries. This must be the case since the rate of surplus value is equal for all industries, but the ratio of constant to variable

---

[32] See Chapter III, above.

capital differs.[33] Prior to the movement of capital to alter this inequality of profit rates, no general rate of profit exists, by definition. Given the a_{ij}'s and L's, the general rate of profit is achieved by changes in prices. Price changes result in the redistribution of surplus value among industries, and, ideally, this process ends when the same rate of profit prevails in each industry. In the two-industry case, this must involve prices rising in the industry that has the higher ratio of constant to variable capital, and prices falling in the other. In the case of many industries, the realistic case, it is not possible to predict the direction of price movement for any given industry, whatever its value composition of capital.[34]

It appears that the movement of capital determines the profit rate, while in fact this movement establishes the social average as the general. Competition is the mechanism by which capital as a whole devolves into its component parts.[35] This same process, which creates a general rate of profit across industries, brings about uneven development within industries. In the abstract, one can conceive of the movement of capital between industries for a given development of the productive forces in each industry (given the a_{ij}'s and L's). However, in the process of accumulation this movement is the process of the introduction of new techniques, so that the invasion of capital into a branch of industry with a high rate of profit revolutionizes the productive forces there. This creates a stratification of capitals in each industry and unequal profit rates within the industry, as the more efficient capitals capture a larger share of the surplus value realized as profit in that industry.

Thus, the process of the equalization of the rate of profit among industries is also the process of uneven development and stratification within industries. Competition tends to equalize returns by industry and also to generate unequal re-

[33] That is, the value composition of capital—the ratio of the value of the means of production to the value of labor power.

[34] Sraffa, *The Production of Commodities by Means of Commodities* (Cambridge, England: Cambridge University Press, 1973).

[35] See *Capital*, III, Part II.

turns within industries. It is a mistake, therefore, to conceive of competition as an equilibrating mechanism, for it establishes not a stable, sustainable relationship among capitals, but rather a general rate of profit among industries. The tendency for the rate of profit to equalize hides a fiercely competitive struggle within industries between the strong and the weak.

The law of value predicts a tendency for profit rates to equalize among industries. It shares this prediction with bourgeois theory. But the latter treats this tendency as a process of establishing general equilibrium by ignoring stratification of capitals within industries (the "representative firm" assumption). The same tendency in value theory is a mechanism of disequilibrium, creating an unstable and fragile, uneven development among competitors. This aspect of the law of value is central to our discussion of crises in Chapter VIII.

CHAPTER VII

FIXED CAPITAL AND
CIRCULATION

A. THE CIRCULATION OF CAPITAL

Capitalist society is based upon the exploitation of labor through the buying and selling of labor power. The existence of labor power as a commodity implies not only the capital relation but the circulation of capital. Since money is advanced to initiate production, realization must follow production so that the process can be started afresh. Overall, this process of circulation appears irrational, in that it seems that value expands as money, M-M', since these are the terminal points from the point of view of capital. It appears that the expansion of value is not material, in that the terminal points, M and M' appear as only quantitatively different amounts of money. To this point, we have largely considered circulation as the circulation of value, with little analysis of the material process that is the basis of this circulation. In order to proceed further and consider the cause of economic crises, we must treat the basis of circulation, production itself. The circulation of capital has three moments, as we have seen, associated with three forms of capital—money capital, productive capital, and commodity capital. These must be considered in detail—and the relationship between them—in order to relate the circulation of value to the circulation of use values. In this dual circulation arises the contradiction that generates crises.

The circuit of capital presupposes the general circulation of commodities and, in particular, that labor power be a commodity. The initial moment in the circuit, M-C, represents a historically unique way of uniting the means of production with the laborer.[1] Of the three moments in the circuit of capital, this is the one that identifies the circuit as a circuit of capital. The sale of labor power gives this mode of production its particular character and exists under no other mode of production. It is followed by the moment of production, during which capital exists as productive capital, capital as function. The moment of production is not unique to capitalism. Human effort and the objects of labor have been combined in production in all societies in order to produce objects of use. What makes a labor process capitalist in nature, and what stamps the productive forces as capital, is the particular manner in which they enter the production process. It is during the production process that new value is produced, in the material form of use values. Once produced, these use values must be transformed into money, C'-M'. Failure to do so necessarily implies that the circuit cannot be renewed at a higher level. The last step involves the return of capital to its purely social form (money), the form in which it is again a claim on commodities in most general form.

The circuit of capital, when taken as M-$C \ldots P \ldots C'$-M', is a circuit of replacement, the replacement of specific value (commodities) for general value, then the replacement of the means of production and labor power, to initiate production again. In this chapter we consider this process of replacement and re-initiation in detail.

B. FIXED AND CIRCULATING CAPITAL

To initiate production, capitalists advance money in two parts, constant capital and variable capital. These two categories of advanced capital correspond to two functions in the

---

[1] More completely, $M \underset{\diagdown}{\overset{\diagup}{}}$ CC — means of production / VC — labor power

Where CC denotes constant capital and VC = variable capital, exchanged against the means of production and labor power, respectively.

production process. Constant capital exchanges for the means of production, commodities whose value is transferred in the production process from one material object to another. The means of production are constant capital because their value remains constant in production. A certain amount of steel, coal, machinery, etc., enters production representing a certain value. After production has occurred, this value is embodied in newly produced commodities. Labor power also enters the production process with a certain value, but the consumption of labor power in production results in expanded value. Therefore, the money exchanged for labor power is variable capital, in that value created varies from the value that enters the labor process. Variable capital is "variable" in another sense, which reflects the domination of capital over the production process. When a capitalist buys steel, for example, the consumption of that steel is given by or constant relative to the techniques of production. Without a change in technology affecting the amount of steel in the commodities to be produced, or without a degrading of the quality of these commodities, a certain amount of steel allows for the production of a certain number of commodities. This is not the case with labor power. A capitalist may purchase the capacity to work of a given number of laborers for a specific length of time, but the intensity of work is not determined until product occurs. Capitalists, or their supervisory agents on the shop floor, can obtain a varying amount of effort from workers. Indeed, the intensity of work, like the length of the working day, is the product of day-to-day class struggle. In capitalism's early stages, the intensity of work is primarily determined by the oppression and coercion that capitalists bring to bear on workers on the shop floor. As capitalism matures, this coercion continues, but the introduction of machinery brings the work process increasingly under the direct control of capital and out of the influence of workers, who become increasingly deskilled within machine-paced production processes.[2]

[2] Harry Braverman, *Labor and Monopoly Capital* (New York: Monthly Review, 1974).

The constant capital–variable capital distinction is primary, in that it identifies the source of surplus value. It is a distinction based on the nature of the production of value, a distinction central to the understanding of value and surplus value, but it is of no consequence to capitalists. From the view of operating capitalists, all costs appear the same, and reducing constant capital costs appears just as much a source of profit as reducing labor costs.

When we move from the analysis of the production of value to the circulation of value, the constant capital–variable capital distinction is obscured. Once production has occurred, constant and variable capital are merely two quantities, component parts of the value of a commodity, distinguishable only in an accounting sense. The great bourgeois economists of the eighteenth and nineteenth centuries (Smith and Ricardo) devoted most of their analysis to the circulation of value, and therefore found no necessity to employ the constant capital–variable capital distinction. Rather, they made a distinction between fixed and circulating capital. These categories identify the manner in which the realization of value occurs. Circulating capital includes all of those elements of production that are completely consumed in the production process, and, consequently, whose value circulates with the circulation of the newly produced commodities. These elements are labor power, raw materials, and intermediate commodities. Fixed capital is that part of the means of production that is not completely consumed in production, the part of the value of these means of production that does not circulate but remains fixed ("fixed" Marx sometimes says) in noncirculating material objects such as machines, buildings, etc.

It should be clear that the fixed capital–circulating capital distinction obscures completely the value-creating process, since the source of expanded value (labor power) is lumped together with non-value-expanding means of production. This does not make the concepts invalid; rather it points up their specific and limited usefulness. They are categories for the analysis of the circulation of value. They enter the analysis after production has occurred, presupposing a prior analysis of production and the constant capital–variable capital division. Once the analysis of the production of value has been made, the concepts of fixed and circulating capital allow us to consider the particular problems arising in the circulation and realization of value.

We characterized fixed capital as that part of the means of production which has a life longer than one circuit of capital. This corresponds somewhat, but not precisely, to the neoclassical concept of capital. In neoclassical theory, capital is any element of production that involves deferment of consumption. Thus, a tool that is produced in one period, but whose use exhausted in the next, is capital. An example of neoclassical capital that is excluded from our definition is the proverbial forest.[3] In neoclassical theory, the trees in the forest are capital even if they are all cut down at the same time, since there is a waiting period for the trees to mature. Fixed capital, as we use it, is not characterized by its useful lifespan as such, but by this lifespan in relation to the circuit of capital. The reason for using the definition given above will become clear in our analysis of the circulation of capital.

Fixed capital has two characteristics important for the circulation process. First, the use value of fixed means of production does not circulate, only their value does. Unlike other means of production, fixed means of production undergo no change of material form in the production process. Part of their usefulness is exhausted, but not as a consequence of the material objects being altered. What is transferred to the commodity in the labor process by the consumption of fixed capital is value alone. Second, and obviously related to the first, fixed capital imparts its value to commodities piecemeal, over several production and circu-

---

[3] See William J. Baumol, *Economic Theory and Operations Analysis*. The example of the forest allows within neoclassical theory an apparent case of value-creation without any input of human labor, if the forest is sold prior to the cutting of the trees.

lation cycles.[4] As a consequence, a portion of the value of fixed capital does not circulate, but remains fixated in material form.

This second characteristic lends a special character to the circulation of fixed capital. Since fixed means of production have been purchased with money (they are capital), they must be replaced by a subsequent money purchase when their usefulness is exhausted. Their value is continuously transferred, passed onto the commodities, but they are replaced discretely.[5] This reflects the twofold nature of fixed means of production. As values, they shrink with their material wearing out, and this value is accumulated continuously as money for their replacement. As use values, they are replaced all at once. By reference to concepts previously employed, we can summarize by saying that the transformation of fixed means of production from productive capital to money capital occurs continuously, with the realization of new commodities in money form (money capital). However, the transformation of money capital back into productive capital for these fixed means of production is a separate, discontinuous process. Realization of value and replacement of use value are separate processes.[6] It might seem that we are

---

[4] "[Fixed constant capital] does not circulate in use value form, but it is merely its value that circulates, and this takes place gradually, piecemeal, in proportion as it passes from it to the product, which circulates as a commodity." *Capital*, II, p. 161.

[5] "In the performance of its function that part of the value of an instrument of labor which exists in its bodily form constantly decreases, while that which is transformed into money constantly increases until the instrument of labor is at last exhausted and its entire value, detached from the corpse, is converted into money. Here the particularity in the turnover of this element of productive capital becomes apparent. The transformation of its value into money keeps pace with the pupation into money of the commodity which is the carrier of its value. But its conversion from the money-form into a use value proceeds separately from the reconversion of the commodities into other elements of their production and is determined by its own period of reproduction, that is, by the time during which the instrument of labor wears out." *Ibid.*, p. 166.

[6] "[A] portion of [the] value [of fixed means of production] is continuously circulated and converted into money as a part of the value of the

laboring an obvious point, but in fact the implications of this separation of realization and replacement are not sufficiently recognized.

C. Competition and
the Replacement of Fixed Capital

The nature of fixed capital results in a contradiction between the social process of the realization of value and the material replacement of the means of production. This contradiction involves a conflict between the two processes, which generates economic crises. These crises reflect, in part, the inability to realize the value embodied in fixed means of production. This particular type of realization problem has nothing to do with the inability to realize (convert into money) commodities. Indeed, it is the consequence of the sale of commodities at their values.

As we have seen in Chapter VI, inherent in the circulation of capital is the competition among capitals. Whereas in precapitalist societies competition within the ruling class is carried out in the political sphere, in capitalist society competition is directly economic and occurs through the cheapening of commodities. This cheapening of commodities is achieved through productive innovations, which increase the number of commodities a worker produces per unit of time. Except in trivial cases, productivity is raised by providing workers with new fixed means of production. This development of the productive forces means that at any moment existing means of production are being rendered obsolete.

We must be clear about the manner in which existing means of production are affected. The introduction of a new and more efficient way of making steel has no impact upon the material usefulness of the older methods. To the extent that the latter are not materially exhausted, they remain capable of producing use values (e.g., steel). What is affected

commodities without being reconverted from money into its original bodily form." *Ibid.*, pp. 171-172.

is the ability to pass on their value, to convert it to money form.

If the pressure of competition allows, capitalists with socially obsolete means of production can attempt to continue to stretch the use of those to the limit of their material life. Even if successful in doing so, these capitalists will not be able to realize the value of those means of production. The introduction of new techniques, by reducing the value of commodities, at the same time reduces the value of the old means of production. Marx called this the "moral depreciation of capital," referring to the social process by which useful objects are rendered socially less useful, i.e., less useful in producing surplus value. When rapid technical change is occurring and values are falling rapidly in an industry, materially useful means of production can be rendered socially useless, since they cannot produce commodities at low enough values.

The stratification of capitals in an industry, which we treated in Chapter VI, corresponds to a devaluation of fixed capital, i.e., the impossibility that less efficient capitals will realize the capital they have advanced. This necessarily means that the less efficient capitals cannot realize the surplus value that would fall to them if they were not burdened with socially obsolete means of production. Again, it must be stressed that the failure to realize the value of fixed capital is not because commodities cannot be sold, but because technical change lowers their values.

It should now be clear why fixed capital was defined in terms of how it circulates. In all societies, labor processes have included means of production with a lifespan beyond that of the time necessary to produce use values. This is only the basis of the difference between fixed and circulating capital. The difference itself is the manner in which value is transmitted. In one case, value is transmitted completely and replaced immediately upon resumption of the labor process. In the other case, value is transmitted incrementally and replacement is necessarily deferred. This problem does not arise in precapitalist society, since the means of production are not commodities and do not circulate as values. This manner of transmission of value and character of replacement of use values creates the possibility that conditions may change such that the transmission of value cannot quantitatively correspond to the realization of that value. Competition turns this possibility into actuality.[7]

In summary, fixed capital is fixed in that a part of its value does not circulate through the circuit of capital, while another part is separated from it and circulates with the commodities produced. The conditions of realization for fixed capital are set by the circulation of commodities, and these conditions can render the fixated part of fixed capital unrealizable in whole or part. This reflects a contradiction between the process of production (value transmission) and process of circulation (value realization).[8] In times of economic crisis, this contradiction can bring about catastrophic moral depreciation of capital, and intrinsically useful objects become socially useless.[9]

[7] "This difference in the behavior of the elements of productive capital in the labor-process forms however only the point of departure of the difference between fixed and non-fixed capital, not this difference itself. That follows from the fact alone that this different behavior [material lifespan] exists in equal measure under all modes of production, capitalist and non-capitalist. To this different behavior of material elements corresponds however the *transmission of value* to the product, and to this in turn corresponds the replacement of value by the sale of the product. . . . Hence capital is not called fixed capital because it is fixed in the instruments of labor, but because a part of its value laid out in instruments of labor remains fixed in them, while the other part circulates as a component part of the value of the product." *Ibid.*, pp. 201-202.

[8] "In all these cases the point of issue is *how* a given value, laid out in the process of production of commodities, whether it be wages, the price of raw materials, or that of instruments of labor, is transferred to the product [sphere of production—JW], hence is circulated by the product, and returned to its starting-point by the sale of the product, or is replaced [sphere of circulation—JW]." *Ibid.*, p. 230.

[9] "[C]ompetition compels the replacement of the old instruments of labor by new ones before the expiration of their material life, especially when decisive changes occur. Such premature renewals of factory equipment on a rather large social scale are mainly enforced by catastrophes or crises." *Ibid.*, p. 174.

We can now see that though the realization of value appears as a quantitative problem, it is in fact a problem of qualitative changes that accompany accumulation. The problem appears quantitative insofar as it is viewed simply as the matching of a certain quantity of commodity capital with an equal amount of money capital. Since the commodity capital reaches the market with its value determined, the concordance between this amount and the money capital it will exchange against seems to be determined by the latter. This, of course, is the view of the "underconsumptionist" school, which analyzes realization in terms of what determines the demand of commodities (represented by money capital).

Were there no fixed capital, the realization of value would be a quantitative issue alone. Capital advanced for production would circulate in its entirety in commodities, and the realization of these commodities would be the realization of capital advanced for any circuit of capital. Realization of value, in part or whole, would correspond to the money exchanged for commodities. In this case the circulation of value would proceed smoothly. Any interruption of this circulation would have to be explained by factors influencing the moment C'-M' itself, not by the moment of production.

But the existence of fixed capital introduces a qualitative element into the analysis of circulation. The realization of circulating capital can be considered purely quantitatively, for the sale of commodities at their values assures the conversion of the value of circulating capital into money. But since technical change reduces the values of commodities, an equality of value produced and value realized does not ensure a realization of the value of fixed capital.

D. Durability of Fixed Capital
and Capitalist Development

The specific character of the realization and replacement of fixed capital becomes increasingly contradictory as capitalism develops. Technical change is brought about by the competitive struggle among capitals. The intention of capitalists in introducing technical changes is to lower the unit cost of production and raise their rate of profit. Let us represent the unit cost of production of a commodity as $CC + VC$, which Marx called the "cost-price." For a capitalist, this sum represents a brenchmark, in that it is the minimum selling price at which the capital he advances for the commodity will be replaced by money. In fact, to the capitalist $CC + VC$ appears as the basis of price, rather than a mere component part of the value of the commodity.[10] Indeed, in this simple cost calculation, "the extortion of surplus labor loses its specific character."[11] As we have seen (Chapter III), surplus value is distributed on the basis of capital advanced, so it appears that constant capital is as much a source of profit as variable capital. This inversion of reality equates the calculation of profit with the source of profit.[12]

The nature of fixed capital requires an expansion of the cost price formula in order to analyze the two qualitatively different aspects of constant capital, i.e. $(CC_1 + CC_2) + VC$, where CC_1 represents the transfer of value from fixed means of production and CC_2 the transferred value of raw materials and intermediate commodities. As noted, CC_1 represents the transfer of value alone, while CC_2 represents a transfer of value corresponding to the actual material transformation of means of production.

In capitalist society, the introduction of technical change is determined by the impact of technical change on the cost price, i.e., on the process of value transfer. This impact on

---

[10] "The minimal limit of the selling price of a commodity is its cost price. If it is sold under its cost price, the expended constituent elements of productive capital cannot be fully replaced out of the selling price. If this process continues, the value of the advanced capital disappears. From this point of view alone, the capitalist is inclined to regard the cost price as the true *inner* value of the commodity, because it is the price required for the bare conservation of his capital." *Ibid.*, p. 38.

[11] *Capital*, III, p. 45.

[12] "This way in which surplus value is transformed into the form of profit by way of the rate of profit is, however, a further development of the inversion of subject and object that takes place already in the process of production." *Ibid.*, p. 45.

value transfer reflects changes in the material process of production, and the analysis of technical change and production provides the basis for the analysis of the production and transfer of value.

The ability of people to produce use values is determined by the means of production at their disposal, their quantity and quality. Increases in the mass of use values produced per unit of time are achieved by increasing the fixed means of production employed by labor. This increase in the technical composition of production—the number of workers to fixed means of production—comes about through the division of labor. In modern bourgeois theory this rise in the ratio of means of production to labor power is called "capital deepening," and, to the extent it is analyzed at all, is treated purely quantitatively. This is because the production process is considered only from the value side, which abstracts from the material process involved.

Changes in the productivity of labor are achieved through division of labor within the production process. Marx, of course, did not discover this fact, for it is the basis of Adam Smith's theory of technical change.[13] Marx's contribution was that he related this division of labor to the process of value production under capitalist relations. The division of labor within production is achieved by the introduction of machinery, which reduces and simplifies the tasks performed by each worker. As a consequence, the division of labor within production is the process of the de-skilling of the proletariat.[14] The concrete skills of the laborer become increasingly degraded and irrelevant, so that the formal abstraction from concrete labor in exchange becomes a real abstraction in production. Through the division of tasks, tasks become trivialized to the point that each worker is a virtual substitute for every other in production as well as exchange.

The process of technical change necessarily involves providing each worker with more fixed means of production.

[13] Smith used the example of a pin factory to demonstrate how the division of labor increases productivity.

[14] *Capital*, I, Chapter XV.

This is a controversial conclusion, attacked by bourgeois critics of the labor theory of value, who argue that technical change can be "capital saving,"[15] by which they mean "constant capital saving." If we completely abstract from the material aspect of the production process, it is certainly possible to posit such an outcome. The cost price has two elements, CC and VC, and if we are oblivious to how technical change actually occurs, we can say that its result is either to decrease constant capital ("capital saving") or variable capital ("labor saving"). Certainly these two possibilities exist in the realm of ideas, though it is rather like shooting an arrow into the air blindfolded and concluding that one has a fifty-fifty chance of hitting a bird—either one will or one won't.

At the moment we in fact are not arguing about the effect of technical change on the ratio of constant capital to variable capital, but the impact upon the ratio of the mass of the means of production to the mass of labor power; that is, we are considering the material (use value) side. The argument is that the division of labor in production is achieved by the introduction of machinery, which subdivides and simplifies tasks. If other things remain unchanged, the introduction of more machinery will raise the ratio of constant to variable capital (the organic composition of capital). Since living labor is the source of expanded value, this would tend to reduce the rate of profit.[16] One way of overcoming this tendency is to increase the durability of fixed means of production. If fixed means of production are made to last longer, the portion of their value that they transfer to commodities during any production period is reduced. Let us consider the

[15] See Geoff Hodgson, "The Theory of the Falling Rate of Profit," *New Left Review*, 84 (1974).

[16] The average rate of profit for a given time period is

$$\frac{N(SV)}{K + N(CC + VC)},$$

where K is the non-circulating amount of capital (fixed capital) and N the number of production periods over the time span for which the rate of profit is measured.

cost price of a commodity, $CC + VC$. A technical change that involved nothing more than increasing the material lifespan of fixed capital (while allowing the same number of commodities to be produced each production period) would reduce the constant capital portion of the cost price.

Thus in capitalist society, competition generates a tendency to lengthen the physical lifespan of fixed means of production as one way of reducing cost price. This tendency is in direct contradiction with the struggle among capitals, which forces the shortening of the value life of fixed means of production.[17] To counteract downward pressure on profitability, capitalists seek innovations that extend the material usefulness of fixed means of production. But this extended material life of constant capital is contradicted by the competition among capitals, which continually shortens the social lifespan of fixed means of production. This contradiction intensifies as capitalism develops, and is perhaps the clearest example of what Marx identified as the general conflict between the development of the productive forces, on the one hand, and the relations of production, on the other. This contradiction generates devaluation of socially obsolete fixed capital, making its conversion into money capital (realization) quantitatively incomplete. On the other hand, the same competitive forces induce a lengthening of the material life of fixed means of production. In capitalist society, competition induces the longevity of fixed capital and, at the same time, contradicts that longevity by devaluing fixed capital. This devaluation, which is the result of accumulation itself, makes economic crises inherent in capitalism, crises during which the devaluation of fixed capital brings on the general devaluation of commodities. It is this process that we consider in the next chapter.

[17] "Whereas the development of fixed capital extends the length of this [material] life on the one hand, it is shortened on the other by the continuous revolution in the means of production, which likewise incessantly gains momentum with the development of the capitalist mode of production." *Capital*, II, p. 188.

CHAPTER VIII

ACCUMULATION
AND CRISES

A. Economic Crises

A repeated theme in the foregoing chapters has been that capitalist society is based upon historically unique relations of production and that these social relations manifest themselves in forms that assume a unique character. While some of them are older than capitalism—money and commodities, for example—they take on new and qualitatively different significance in capitalist society. As a consequence, all of the phenomena considered to this point—value, profit, money, credit, competition, and fixed means of production—present themselves not in isolation, not as abstract topics for treatment, but as part of the circulation of capital. These phenomena, considered in this context, interact to generate the most concrete manifestation of the historical uniqueness of capitalism, namely economic crises.

By an economic crisis we mean an interruption or disjuncture in the process of social reproduction that involves the incomplete reproduction of the circuit of capital. An economic crisis is the same thing as capitalist crisis, or a crisis of capital, since the category "economic" presupposes bourgeois society and capitalist social relations. As argued in Chapter II, the division of social life into the economic and the non-economic reflects the twofold nature of commodities, so that labor performed for exchange becomes subject to objective regulation in the phenomenal form of monetary costs. In this way, it is formally separated from all other labor performed for other reasons. This separation remains incomplete until labor power itself is a commodity, in which case each working person's life is institutionally divided be-

tween work (the economic) and leisure (the non-economic).
From this division emerge the categories of bourgeois society—wages, profit, etc.—which are the surface expressions
of capital's domination of social production. The term "economic crisis" presupposes these categories, just as the phenomenon it refers to presupposes the circulation of capital.

One could use the term "economic crisis" to refer to any
interruption in social reproduction that had its origin in the
material process of production. For example, it could be used
to describe the consequences of the Black Death in medieval
Europe, since the plague resulted in declines of production,
widespread dislocation of population, and famine. However,
to do so would render the term "economic" meaningless in
theory, as well as contradict what is generally understood by
identifying a crisis as "economic." At least since the time of
Ricardo, economic crisis has referred to the phenomenon of
overproduction, a situation in which use values pile up idle,
unused.[1] Crises of overproduction necessarily involve overproduction of value, in which some commodities cannot be
sold, and realization is the necessary condition for their consumption as use values. From our previous discussion (Chapter
II), we see that overproduction of value implies overproduction of capital, since commodities (the carriers of objectified labor) are commodity capital.

As long as products do not circulate as commodities but
are produced directly for consumption without the media-
tion of exchange, overproduction of use values is impossible.
Interruptions in social reproduction in precapitalist society
took the form of underproduction of use values, resulting in
famine, social upheavals, and so on, and were themselves the
result of plagues, warfare, natural disasters, or direct class
conflicts that undermined the relation of the exploited to the
exploiter.[2] All meaning of the term "economic" is lost if

[1] For a discussion of why Adam Smith did not deal with the problem of
general overproduction, see Karl Marx, *Theories of Surplus Value* (Moscow:
Progress Publishers, 1968), Book II, pp. 484ff.

[2] See Robert Brenner, "The Origins of Capitalist Development: A Critique of Neo-Smithian Marxism," *New Left Review*, 104 (July-August 1977).

such crises are categorized with the form of social disruption unique to capitalism, general overproduction of use values.

Any theory of capitalist reproduction with a pretension to be seriously considered must account for economic crises.[3] Marx's entire mature works were devoted to explaining economic crises, and his theory of crisis is inseparable from his theory of accumulation. In the process of accumulation, all of the tensions and contradictions of capitalist production and circulation are intensified, and economic crisis is the necessary outcome of the accumulation process.[4] Prior to considering economic crises, we must analyze the process of accumulation. In doing so, we integrate the various elements treated in previous chapters.

B. Accumulation and Value Formation

Capitalist accumulation is a particular historical form of social reproduction in which the material reproduction of the means of production and means of subsistence occurs in a manner to produce a specific form of class rule (the dictatorship of the bourgeoisie) and a specific form of exploitation of the direct producer. If we take the conditions for capital's existence as given, accumulation is the duplication of the capital-labor relationship on an expanding scale. For this reason, Marx at one point defines accumulation as the growth of the proletariat.[5] In countries where there are significant precapitalist sectors, accumulation involves the transformation of direct producers from servile and petty commodity production relations into proletarians, a qualitative transformation of the relations of production. In advanced capitalist countries, the growth of the proletariat is achieved by the replenishing and depletion of the industrial reserve army,

---

[3] For a brief survey of crisis theories, bourgeois and Marxist, see Anwar Shaikh, "A History of Crisis Theories," URPE, *U.S. Capitalism in Crisis* (New York: Union of Radical Political Economists, 1977).

[4] *Capital*, III, Chapter XV.

[5] *Capital*, I, p. 576.

which Marx called "the general law of capitalist accumulation,"[6] a law considered below.

Since living labor is the source of value, the growth of the employed proletariat implies the expansion of value, so capitalist accumulation is the accumulation of value.[7] Considered purely as the accumulation of value, capitalist accumulation appears as a quantitative phenomenon, M-C-M', $M' > M$. It is not uncommon for accumulation to be treated as if this were its essential character, rather than merely its appearance.[8] For some purposes it is useful to analyze the purely quantitative aspect of accumulation, but in doing so it is not accumulation that is being treated but expanded reproduction.[9]

In Chapter VII we noted that if one abstracts from fixed capital (and, therefore, from technical change), the realization of value becomes a purely quantitative question. Therefore, expanded reproduction, which makes precisely these abstractions, is the vehicle by which one can analyze the quantitative aspect of realization. Marx created this idealized framework—expanded reproduction—to do exactly this.[10] But these abstractions cannot be made if accumulation is to be treated. Expanded reproduction should not be thought of as a simplified model of accumulation, but as an idealized construct to demonstrate the quantitative aspects of the circuit of capital, in which the mechanics of realization are demonstrated, so that when we turn to accumulation we can eliminate realization as a cause of the interruption of accu-

---

[6] *Ibid*, Chapter XXV.

[7] Value—and surplus value—can increase even with a constant or declining employed proletariat, though newly created value cannot (assuming a given working day and intensity of labor). Total value would increase if the ratio of dead to living labor (CC/VC) rose with a constant employed proletariat. Since, as we shall see, this implies a rise in the rate of surplus value once new values are established, total surplus value would rise.

[8] See M. Itoch, "A Formulation of Marx's Theory of Crisis," *Science and Society* 42 (Summer 1978).

[9] See Weeks, "Process of Accumulation and the 'Profit Squeeze' Hypothesis," *Science and Society* (Fall 1979).

[10] *Capital*, Vol. II, Chapter XXI.

mulation.[11] By proceeding on the assumption that commodities are realized at their values, we are not assuming away problems of realization, but moving them from the category of causes to the category of consequences.

While accumulation is the process of value expansion, it is simultaneously the process of value formation. The first can be considered in terms of capital-as-a-whole, while the latter involves the interaction of many capitals. As we pointed out in Chapter VI, Marx first analyzed accumulation by abstracting from competition among capitals. The basis for accumulation is the production of surplus value, which takes place in the context of the competition between the two great classes of bourgeois society, the capitalist class and the proletariat. This competition, or class struggle, underlies the quantitative expansion of capital. The qualitative developments within this quantitative expansion reflect the competition among industrial capitals and between industrial and money capital.

Inherent in the capital relation is competition among capitals or the fragmentation of total capital into formally autonomous parts, which is the same thing. This competition manifests itself in the cheapening of commodities, achieved by technical change. Of the many elements of accumulation, perhaps technical change is that most mystified by bourgeois political economy. This mystification has two aspects. Conceptually, it is mystified by being treated only from the value side, which we discussed in the context of fixed capital. A second aspect of mystification is the manner in which technical change is viewed temporally. It is characteristically treated as a long run influence, whose consequences can be ignored in the short run, where the latter coincides with the "business cycle."[12] First, the "short run–long run" distinction in bourgeois theory has nothing to do with the passage

[11] Shaikh's discussion of the underconsumptionist hypothesis explains this. See Anwar Shaikh, "A History of Crisis Theories."

[12] See Howard Sherman, "A Marxian Theory of the Business Cycle," *Review of Radical Political Economics*, 11 (Spring 1979).

of time, but refers to abstract analytical categories.[13] At any moment some capitals are introducing new production techniques, and while these can be bunched at certain moments, they occur continuously. Likewise, their impact is felt continuously, though obviously the impact of technical change increases with the passage of time. But since long time periods are made up of small time periods, it is totally contradictory to ignore technical change during the latter and consider it during the former, since the one is the sum of the others. As we shall see, this metaphysical temporal distinction results in a misunderstanding and distortion of the tendency of the rate of profit to fall.

As accumulation proceeds, the competition among capitals leads to the introduction of new techniques of production. Capitalists are so motivated in order to reduce unit costs of production. However this is achieved technically, it involves a fall in the value of commodities, so that the concrete labor time necessary to produce a commodity falls in those production units where the new techniques have been introduced. Thus technical change creates a quantitative indeterminacy in the value (socially necessary abstract labor time) of commodities. Except in the idealized neoclassical world of the "representative firm," technical changes are not introduced throughout an industry,[14] but in a few capitals only. If we consider one industry, technical change creates a situation in which the same commodity is produced with different amounts of concrete labor.

The importance of the analysis of value (in Chapters I and

[13] In neoclassical theory, the short run is the period over which the firm is locked into a given plant and equipment, and the long run the period during which fixed means of production ("plant") can be varied. Whatever the analytical use of this distinction, it is irrelevant to the actual passage of time (as neoclassical theorists point out). The long run exists only as a concept, which is why "long-run cost curves" are often called "planning curves."

[14] Neoclassical theory formally recognizes this problem of many techniques for the same commodity in "vintage-capital" models. However, it remains true that the general theory of neoclassical economics is developed by abstracting from many techniques to the "representative firm."

II) should now become clear. If we hold to an embodied labor view of value, our theory of value would break down at this point, since we are faced with a situation in which a commodity reaches the market after being produced with different amounts of concrete labor. Neo-Ricardians argue that in such a situation it is not possible to define the value of a commodity, and, given their definition of value, they are correct. When there are many techniques of production, the labor embodied in a commodity is conceptually indeterminate. [15]

We are presented with the conceptual problem of constructing a single value for a commodity out of a diversity of labor processes. This conceptual problem reflects a real indeterminacy, an indeterminacy resolved by the competition among capitals. In the circulation of commodities, some of the capitalists discover that part of the concrete labor consumed under their domination is not socially necessary, i.e., part of it is not value creating (in the case of living labor). [16] This discovery is made upon the sale of the commodity and is presented as an objective fact in the market price of the commodity. The process of value formation presents us with the category to resolve our conceptual problem, namely objectified labor. The value of a commodity is not determined by the concrete labor consumed in its production in a particular labor process, but the concrete labor of all labor process for one commodity transformed into abstract (objectified) labor by the interaction of many capitals in exchange.

[15] See Ian Steedman, *Marx after Sraffa* (London: New Left Books, 1977). Even speaking of embodied labor presupposes a homogeneity of concrete labors within a labor process.

[16] "[S]ince the circulation process of capital is not completed in one day but extends over a fairly long period until the capital returns to it original form, since this period coincides with the period within which market-prices equalize with [prices of production—JW], and great upheavals and changes take place in the productivity of labor and therefore also in the *real value* of commodities." *Theories of Surplus Value*, II, p. 495.

In the original, Marx wrote "cost prices" where I have inserted "prices of production." Since cost price does not include profit, he obviously meant "prices of production."

The process of accumulation involves the initiation of the circuit of capital upon the basis of one set of values, and the generation of a new set of values that confronts capitalists at the end of the circuit. The moments of circulation, $M\text{-}C$ and $C'\text{-}M'$ are the moments when changes in the material process of production manifest themselves as changes in values. What appears as purely quantitative, $M\text{-}C(\ .\ .\ .\ P\ .\ .\ .\ )C'\text{-}M'$ is the phenomenal form of continuous qualitative change. The change of form of capital (money capital to productive capital to commodity capital) is the process of the formation of new values.[17] This necessarily implies, given the working day and intensity of labor, that the circulation of capital affects the amount of surplus value that can be realized as profit (since surplus value is part of total value).

The impact of the formation of a new value for a particular commodity is not, of course, limited to that branch of industry. If the commodity is a means of production, a decline in its value directly cheapens the constant capital in every branch of industry using that commodity as an input, which reduces all those commodities in value. If the commodity is an element of workers' consumption, a decline in its value reduces the value of labor power and may cheapen variable capital.[18] Thus technical change, even if restricted to a few commodities (though there is no reason to assume it to be so) results in a general devaluation of commodities in the process of accumulation.

The formation of new values, subsumed within accumulation, involves the process of the redistribution of capital (centralization) as well as the growth of existing capitals

[17] "The *comparison* of value in one period with the value of the same commodities in a later period is no scholastic illusion . . . but rather forms the fundamental principle of the circulation process of capital." *Theories of Surplus Value*, II, p. 495.

[18] A decline in the value of the means of subsistence need not cheapen variable capital if the standard of living of the working class rises. These are two separate processes—one of involving the adjustment of unit values (competition among capitals), the other the adjustment of material consumption (competition between labor and capital). Their relationship to each other is complex. See John Weeks, "Process of Accumulation."

(concentration). In consequence, analysis of accumulation requires treatment of credit as well as competition among capitals. The introduction of new technology involves, as we
have seen, an increased division of labor, requiring production on an expanded scale. The growth of credit proceeds
along with accumulation, so that the pyramiding of financial
obligations goes hand-in-hand with the formation of new
values.

The process of accumulation brings together and unites all
the aspects of capitalism considered previously—the formation of values, the division of money into its functions as
means of circulation and means of payment, the intensifica-
tion of competition, and the contradiction between the
value-life and material-life of fixed capital. The motor force
that is the basis of the interaction of these elements is the
development of the productive forces (technical change).
This development, itself a material process, occurs in the
context of the production of value, and the source of economic crises lies in the opposition of the material and value
aspects of production and circulation,[19] which finds its fullest
expression in the tendency of the rate of profit to fall.

C. The Tendency of the Rate of Profit to Fall

Marx considered the law of the tendency of the rate of profit
to fall to be the most important law of political economy,
and the analysis of it to be the key to unlocking the concrete
workings of a capitalist economy.[20] In *Capital*, we do not

[19] "The contradiction, to put it in a very general way, consists in that the
capitalist mode of production involves a tendency towards absolute development of the productive forces, regardless of the social conditions under
which capitalist production takes place; while, on the other hand, its aim is
to preserve the value of the existing capital and promote its self-expansion
to the highest limit (i.e., to promote an ever more rapid growth of this
value)." *Capital*, III, p. 294.

[20] "This is in every respect the most important law of modern political
economy, and the most essential for understanding the most difficult relations. It is the most important law from the historical standpoint." *Grundrisse*, p. 748.

encounter an exposition of the law until well into volume III. But the tendency in question is clearly present in volume I in the discussion of accumulation.[21] Here all the elements of the tendency are set out. It is not pursued at that point, however, because its implications or consequences cannot be unfolded until one considers the circulation process. In other words, the tendency itself arises in production (the subject of volume I), but the analysis of production is insufficient to give full expression to the tendency.[22] An exposition of the tendency does require abstraction from circulation, however, or its operation becomes lost in manifestation of its consequences.

The tendency of the rate of profit to fall is the direct consequence of the development of the productive forces and, therefore, represents the consequence of the dynamism of capitalist society, the success of capitalism in revolutionizing the forces of production. It is a law (tendencial law) of accumulation, not of stagnation. It is a tendency that emerges in the process of capital-expansion, a dynamic tendency, which disappears when one compares static states.[23]

The circuit of capital is initiated by the exchange of money for the elements of production, $M(CC + VC) - C$. The money advanced is divided into constant and variable capital, and this decision is quantitatively determined by the physical amount of the means of production required in relation to the labor power required, and the value of these. In symbols,[24]

---

[21] *Capital*, I, Chapter XXV.

[22] "The mere (direct) *production process* of capital in itself cannot add anything new in this context [crises]. . . . But [crisis] cannot be shown when dealing with the production process itself, for the latter is not concerned with the *realization* either of the produced value or the surplus value. This can only emerge in the *circulation process* which is in itself also a *process of reproduction*." *Theories of Surplus Value*, II, p. 513.

[23] This will be the basis of our critique of other interpretations of the tendency.

[24] In the text, for simplicity, we assume a single, homogeneous means of production, so that M is a single number (e.g., tons of steel). More generally, M can be defined as a vector of use values and X_M a vector of unit

$$CC = MX_M$$
$$VC = LX_L.$$

Where M = the means of production in units;
  X_M = the unit value of these means of production;
  L = the number of workers, employed for a given time period; and
  X_L = the value of a unit of labor power, for a given time period.

The ratio M/L represents the material proportion in which means of production and labor power are combined, a ratio of use values, called the technical composition of capital. This ratio is technical in a limited sense, in that it is a ratio of material components. It is not exclusively determined technically, however, for the techniques of production utilized in any society reflect a process of class struggle. This is particularly true in capitalist society, where the ruling class seeks to establish its control over the direct process of production, and class struggle rages over its ability to do so.

When the means of production are aggregated by use of their values and labor power expressed as a value, the ratio $MX_M/LX_L = CC/VC$ measures the value composition of capital. The tendency of the rate of profit to fall arises from the interaction of the technical and value compositions during the process of accumulation. The relationship between the two is quite complex. Technical change raises the material productivity of labor, so that a given number of workers in a given length of time processes more products. This must necessarily increase the technical composition of capital. This follows as the result of two separable processes. First, increased productivity is achieved by a further division of labor within the work process, as more and more machines each do smaller and more detailed tasks. This involves a rise in the ratio of fixed means of production to the number of workers. As a consequence of this subdivision of the labor

---

values corresponding to the use values. Note that X_L is a number that results from multiplying two vectors, one a vector of use values that workers consume, the other the vector of their values.

process, the number of products produced by a given labor force increases. The circulating means of production that a worker transforms during a given length of time rises. The technical composition of capital rises because of a relative increase in fixed means of production (the cause of productivity increases) and a relative increase in circulating means of production (the consequence of productivity increases).

Whether or not the value composition of capital rises with the development of the forces of production depends upon not only M/L but also V_M and V_L, the values of commodities. What makes the analysis complex is that the same process that increases M/L decreases both V_M and V_L. The complexity has a temporal dimension, since the immediate impact of technical change is to increase M/L, while the adjustment to new (and lower) values must await the process of circulation. We have here an ambiguity in our definition of the value composition of capital. In the phase M-C, labor power and the means of production have been purchases at some set of values. In the subsequent phase, . . . P . . . C' (production), the labor process is altered as a result of technical change, so that when the new commodities are realized (C'-M'), a new set of values will be established. Simply put, at which set of values is M/L to be valorized (aggregated into the value composition of capital)? To accommodate this ambiguity, Marx introduced the concept of the organic composition of capital, which is defined as the value composition calculated prior to the establishment of the new values which are implied (but not yet actualized) by technical change.[25]

Insofar as this distinction between the value and organic compositions is not made, any analysis of accumulation is implicitly static, in that the process of value formation is ig-

[25] After referring to the value and material relationships as we have, Marx writes: "I call the former the *value-composition*, the latter the *technical composition* of capital. Between the two there is a strict correlation. To express this, I call the value-composition of capital, in so far as it is determined by its technical composition and mirrors the changes of the latter, the *organic composition* of capital." *Capital*, I, p. 574.

nored.[26] The distinction reflects a real process and is not merely a measurement question of which set of values to use to convert the technical composition into a value ratio. At one moment in the circuit of capital a set of value relations has been established in the market. A change in the technical composition will result in a devaluation of commodities, but this must await the competition among capitals. To move immediately to the new values is to presuppose the process of value formation; thus, to presuppose accumulation itself. We can describe the process in more detail. The circuit of capital is initiated by the exchange of capital for labor power and the means of production. The values of these were set by the average techniques prevailing in each branch of the economy prior to the exchange. We can call these the "old" values derived from the "old" techniques of production. Those means of production and labor power are then consumed by some capitalists using "new" techniques, which implies lower values in the future. The commodities produced then circulate $(C'-M')$ in a competitive context that lowers their values below the "old" values at which they entered the circuit of capital. It should be clear that technical change necessarily involves a rise in the organic composition of capital, for the organic composition is the technical composition valorized by the old set of values. On the basis of the old values, the rate of surplus value is unchanged, but the ratio of CC/VC has risen. This implies a fall in the rate of profit.[27] Marx called this "the law as such."[28]

[26] To this author's knowledge, the only contemporary writers who both explicitly recognize this distinction and employ it analytically are Fine and Harris in *Re-reading Capital*, Chapter IV. The following discussion builds upon their work.

[27] This follows even if we ignore fixed constant capital in the profit calculation. The average rate of profit is,

$$p = \frac{SV}{CC + VC}$$

$$= \frac{SV/VC}{CC/VC + 1}$$

One must be clear about what has been established at this point. It has not been argued that a rise in the organic composition results in a fall in the average rate of profit (see Chapter III). The law of the tendency of the rate of profit to fall is merely another way of expressing the expelling of living labor from the production process, what Marx called "the general law of capitalist accumulation." Whether or not the tendency results in an actual fall in the average rate of profit, and the average in a fall in the general rate of profit, and, finally, the general in a fall in the rate of industrial profit (e.g., deducting for interest) cannot be considered at this level of abstraction. The movement from the abstract tendency through all the above steps involves the analysis of value formation, which occurs at the level of many capitals. This process of value formation involves a rise in the rate of surplus value, as well as a general devaluation of commodities. Marx was well aware of the tendencial and abstract nature of "the law as such," and set alongside it a second law that encompasses the process of value adjustment—"the law of the counteracting tendencies to the tendency of the rate of profit to fall."[29] The operation of this law of accumulation brings about the adjustments of the value formation process. Changes in the labor process reduce the labor time required to produce commodities. Through the interaction of capitals, this reduces the abstract necessary labor time (value) of commodities. A fall in the value of commodities, given the standard of living of the working class (see Chapter III), reduces the value of labor power. If the working day remains unchanged, this results in a rise in the rate of surplus value. Surplus value is thus raised *relatively*—necessary labor time falls in the context of an unchanged working day. This rise in the rate of surplus value counteracts the tendency of the

---

If CV/VC (the *organic* composition of capital) rises with SV/VC (the rate of surplus value) constant, p must fall.

[28] *Capital*, III, Chapter XIII, "The Law as Such."

[29] *Ibid.*, Chapter XIV.

rate of profit to fall. This counteraction may be reinforced if the values of the means of production fall more than the values of the commodities workers habitually consume. If this occurs, then the value of constant capital may fall relatively to the value of labor power, reducing the value composition of capital; other things equal, this will raise the rate of profit ($SV/CC + VC$, in the simplest case). There is no theoretical reason to believe that technical change would affect the means of production more than the means of consumption, however. So the major aspect of the law of the counteracting tendencies to the tendency of the rate of profit to fall is the increase in the rate of surplus value.

The two laws are closely interrelated, in that the law as such gives rise to its counteracting tendencies. That is, the rise in the technical composition of capital raises labor productivity and lowers the values of commodities. The laws do, however, exist at different levels of abstraction. The law as such arises in production and can be developed for capital-as-a-whole. Since consideration of capitalist production presupposes capitalist relations, the law as such reflects changes in the forces of production. The counteracting tendencies involve the interaction of capitals, and thus the operation of the relations of production (competition, money, credit). When considering the interplay between the tendency and the counteracting tendencies, one is considering a specific example of the conflict between the relations and forces of production.[30]

Nothing distorts the analysis of the relationship between these two laws (tendencial laws) more than interpreting the law as such as a long run phenomenon, though this interpretation is appallingly common.[31] This interpretation confuses the technical composition with its value counterparts. While the historical tendency of capitalist development, a historical tendency continuously realized, is for the technical composition of capital to rise, this expresses nothing more than the

[30] See Fine and Harris, *Re-reading Capital*, Chapter IV.
[31] See Sherman, "A Marxian Theory of the Business Cycle," for example.

development of the productive forces under capitalism. It is merely another way of saying that labor productivity rises. The law as such and its accompanying familiar, the law of counteracting tendencies, are laws of the accumulation process, at work in each circuit of capital. If they are to be placed within a time dimension, then they are indeed short-run laws, laws of value formation.

D. OTHER PRESENTATIONS
OF THE LAW BRIEFLY CONSIDERED

The law as such provides the key to unlocking the dynamics of capitalist crises if one recognizes that it is a law of accumulation. If, on the other hand, it is interpreted not as a dynamic tendency, but as a relationship between static states, it collapses both as an analytical tool and as a descriptive tool. As a consequence, critics of Marx have always sought to present the law statically (as have some defenders of Marx). It is not surprising that the law of the tendency of the rate of profit to fall can be refuted in a static context, for between static states there can be no tendencies, only definitive outcomes. When treating the law as such, critics characteristically omit the word "tendency," referring instead to "the law of the falling rate of profit," a phrase that implies that a prediction has been made as to the actual movement of the rate of profit.[32]

Characteristically, critics present the issue in the form of the following question: can it be demonstrated, given the standard of living of the working class,[33] that one can move analytically from one static equilibrium state with a given rate of profit to another static equilibrium state in which the

[32] An example of this is Hodgson, "The Theory of the Falling Rate of Profit," *New Left Review*, 84 (1974), but the same view is found in Paul Sweezy, *Theory of Capitalist Development* (New York: Monthly Review, 1968). Some defenders of Marx accept this definition of the issue. See David Yaffe, "The Marxian Theory of Crisis, Capital and the State," *Economy and Society* (May 1973).

[33] A rise in the standard of living must be ruled out, since this could cause a fall in the rate of profit with or without any change in the technical composition of capital.

rate of profit is lower? By "static equilibrium" is meant that all commodities circulate at values implied by the most advanced production technique. This question implies a corollary: is there a set of available technical changes which capitalists would choose, which when generally adopted would result in a lower rate of profit?[34] The answer to both questions is irrelevant to the tendency of the rate of profit to fall, though much ink has been spilled debating the answers.

The answers can be summarized briefly. If one assumes that all constant capital turns over in one production period, then the answer to both questions is "no."[35] If one allows for fixed constant capital, then the answer depends upon the assumption made about the ratio of fixed to circulating constant capital over time.[36] We do not pursue these positions here.[37] But whether the answers are affirmative or negative, one has discovered little of interest.

[34] In other words, are there technical changes which lower cost prices (inducing capitalists to adopt them) and subsequently reduce the rate of profit when generally adopted?

[35] The proof of this is sometimes called the "Okishio Theorem." See Nobuo Okishio, "Technical Change and the Rate of Profit," *Kobe University Economic Review*, 7 (1961). For simpler expositions (though still quite technical) see Susan Himmelweit, "The Continuing Saga of the Falling Rate of Profit," *Bulletin*, The Conference of Socialist Economists, 3 (Autumn 1974); and José Alberro and Joseph Persky, "The Simple Analytics of Falling Profit Rates, Okishio's Theorem and Fixed Capital," *Review of Radical Political Economics*, 11 (Fall 1979). In the same vein, but claiming more significance for their conclusions, see John Roemer, "Technical Change and the Tendency of the Rate of Profit to Fall," *Journal of Economic Theory*, 16 (December 1977); Jens Christensen, "Marx and the Falling Rate of Profit," *American Economic Review*, 66 (May 1976); and Phillippe Van Parijs, "The Falling-Rate-of-Profit Theory of Crisis: A Rational Reconstruction by Way of Obituary," *Review of Radical Political Economics*, 12 (Spring 1980). The title of the last article brings to mind Samuel Clemens's reaction to reading his own obituary in the press: "The reports of my death are highly exaggerated."

[36] Shaikh gets a fall in the rate of profit by appropriate assumptions. See Anwar Shaikh, "Political Economy and Capitalism—Notes on Dobb's Theory of Crisis," *Cambridge Journal of Economics*, 2 (1978).

[37] The static falling rate of profit issue is treated in Ben Fine and John Weeks, "Recent Criticism of the Law of the Tendency of the Rate of Profit to Fall" (Washington: MS, 1980).

The law as such and the counteracting tendencies to it are, as we have seen, not laws of long run development, but laws of accumulation. They come into play as a result of a dynamic process of uneven development and disappear when one considers static positions. To try to refute or defend the law of the tendency of the rate of profit to fall by reference to situations in which commodities exchange at equilibrium values is like trying to analyze the acceleration of bodies by gravity when they are lying at rest. The phenomenon is defined out of existence.

One of the most common formulations of the falling rate of profit is to say that the rate of profit will fall if the organic composition of capital rises more than the rate of surplus value as the result of technical change.[38] This view is also static. First, it can be shown that this cannot in fact occur if one abstracts from fixed constant capital. Second, the two changes (in CC/VC and SV/VC) are part of the same process of value formation and are therefore related to each other in a strict and determinate way, so that the statement collapses into "the rate of profit will fall if the rate of profit falls." Marx, in fact, does consider in detail the relationship between the rate of surplus value and the composition of capital, but does so by use of the distinction between the value composition and the organic composition, which renders the analysis dynamic.[39]

E. The Tendency of the Rate of Profit to Fall and Value Formation

The tendency of the rate of profit to fall manifests itself as an actual fall in the average rate of profit as a result of the

[38] Sweezy, *Theory of Capitalist Development.*

[39] In the three chapters on the law and its operation (Vol. III, Chapters XIII-XV), the terminology is not always precise, which reflects the fact that Marx did not live to revise these chapters. Indeed, he did not even set the order of Vol. III, this being the work of Engels. However, from the discussion it is clear that Marx carried forward the organic-value distinction he had made in Vol. I.

process of value formation. The tendency is actualized as a result of the quantitative difference between the values that prevail when capital is advanced and those that prevail upon the realization of commodities. In other words, the process of accumulation has within it the devaluation of existing capital. In analyzing this process, we must draw together all our previous discussions, for the contradictions associated with them reach their most intense manifestation in the tendency of the rate of profit to fall. In order to explain adequately this process, we must consider not only why the average rate of profit should fall but also why it should *not* under certain circumstances.[40] If the rate of profit always fell, it would not be a tendency, but an inevitable trend. Further, if it in all circumstances fell, accelerated accumulation would be impossible, for in each circuit of capital, the ratio of surplus value to capital advanced would fall. Since accumulation is the result of capitalized surplus value, a falling rate of profit would imply a secular slowdown in accumulation in all capitalist countries. The task, then, is to explain both why the rate of profit does fall and why under some circumstances it does not. A theory that always predicts one or the other is no guide to understanding reality, where *both* occur.

Accumulation is initiated by the advancing of capital, and the elements of production are purchased at some set of prevailing values. Further, production occurs on the basis of workers employing a quantity of fixed means of production purchased at some set of values. Technical change reduces living labor relatively to the means of production, raising the organic composition of capital. Once the production process is completed, the produced commodities must be realized. Since technical change does not occur evenly, different capitals bring the same commodities to the market after using different quantities of concrete labor in their production. In the process of realization, new values are objectified in these commodities, lower than before.

[40] Yaffe, for example, fails to demonstrate this, and his analysis implies that the rate of profit would always fall. Yaffe, "Marxian Theory of Crisis."

This results in two major consequences. First, within each branch of industry, a redistribution of surplus value occurs. Those capitals unaffected by technical change will have higher cost prices than those which have introduced the new technique. As a consequence, at the uniform selling price, the former will realize less surplus value as profit than the latter. For the less efficient capitals, the rate of profit will fall. This fall in the rate of profit for these capitals is the result of having initiated the circuit of capital at one set of values and realizing their commodities at a second, lower, set of values. But this is also true of the innovating capitals, and leads to the second effect. For all capitals, the realization values are below the initial values, so that the capital advanced (denominator of the profit formula) is calculated upon values that are higher than the values that determine the amount of surplus value realized. The greater the increase in the productivity of labor, the greater will be the quantitative difference between these two sets of values.

During this process, it is the organic composition of capital that is relevant, since the new and lower set of values does not affect capital advanced until the next circuit of capital, when it enters the profit calculation. But even at that point, the new values only affect increments of fixed capital, for all fixed capital that has been bought at previous values does not circulate in its entirety; part remains "fixated." The problem for capital is to realize the existing means of production in the context of the progressive devaluation of those means of production.[41] This problem affects those capitals using new means of production as well as those using socially obsolete ones. For each capital means of production and labor power are purchased at one set of values and realized at another. The difference is that for the capitals using new means of production, the devaluation of advanced cap-

---

[41] "In reproduction, just as in the accumulation of capital, it is not only a question of replacing *the same* quantity of use-values of which capital consists on the former scale or an enlarged scale . . . but of replacing the *value* of the capital advanced along with the usual rate of profit (surplus-value)." *Theory of Surplus Value*, II, p. 494.

ital is offset in part or whole by the reduction in the cost price of the realized commodities.

In this process of accumulation and value formation, the rate of profit will fall for some capitals, namely those using old means of production. As the circuits of capital repeat themselves, each time with technical change reducing the concrete labor consumed in the production of commodities, the stratification of capitals will increase. The number of capitals experiencing a fall in the rate of profit depends upon the intensity of the competitive struggle. Consider the case of two sets of capitals, one using old means of production and another (generally larger) using new means of production. We say "generally larger" because the process of technical change involves an increased division of labor in the labor process, which implies a larger scale of production. Each labor process, its productivity determined by the vintage of its means of production, implies a different set of equilibrium values. When the commodities produced by each process reach the market, they must be realized at a common value. The closer the unit realization value is to the old value, the smaller will be the devaluation of capital advanced and vice versa. So, a fierce competitive struggle that forces down realized value toward the value implied by the new means of production can reduce realized surplus value (profit) for all capitals, i.e., generate a general fall in the rate of profit (though this general fall affects the more efficient capitals less).

To this point, we have said nothing about crises, only argued that technical change, by devaluing existing means of production, can under certain circumstances result in a fall in the rate of profit, differentially affecting various capitals. This process is the consequence of the simultaneous existence of means of production of different efficiencies in terms of use of concrete labor. If we abstract from this stratification of capitals and consider only equilibrium situations, where the same values prevail when capital is advanced and when commodities are realized, no fall in the rate of profit, general or specific, occurs. In such a case, we are dealing only with the value composition of capital, abstracting from accumulation itself.

F. Crises and the Tendency of
the Rate of Profit to Fall

Capitalist reproduction is an integrated process of social production and circulation, and its repetition involves the unity of these two moments. A crisis in such a society manifests itself as the disunity or separation of these two moments. The possibility of such a separation is inherent in the unity itself, since the unity is an antagonistic one.[42] This antagonism manifests itself at the most abstract level in the metamorphosis of the commodity itself, C-M. This metamorphosis expresses nothing more than the fact that a commodity is produced for its exchange value, but this simple fact allows for the possibility that, once produced, it may not be exchangeable.[43]

The moment of circulation, C-M, cannot provide us with the explanation of crisis. In the main, commodities are converted into money, and the task is to explain why in most cases the transformation C-M occurs and in other cases it does not. The exchange itself cannot explain this, but only indicate after the fact that realization of commodities was or was not possible.[44] The metamorphosis of commodities oc-

[42] "The *possibility* of crisis, which became apparent in the *simple metamorphosis* of the commodity, is once more demonstrated, and further developed, by the disjunction between the (direct) process of production and the process of circulation. As soon as these processes do not merge smoothly into one another but become independent of one another, the crisis is there." *Ibid.*, p. 507.

[43] "The *most abstract form of crisis* (and therefore the formal possibility of crisis) is thus the *metamorphosis of the commodity* itself; the contradiction of exchange value and use value, and furthermore of money and commodity." *Ibid.*, p. 508.

[44] "The factors which turn this possibility of crisis into [an actual] crisis are not contained in this form itself; it only implies that the *framework* for a crisis exists." *Ibid.*, III, p. 508.

curs not in isolation, but as part of the circuit of capital, and it is in the circuit of capital that the explanation of crisis lies.

As we have seen, the process of accumulation involves a redistribution of social labor among branches of industry. This redistribution of labor implies a redistribution of surplus value, so that individual capitals may expand beyond the limit set by their realized profit. This involves the socialization of capital and is facilitated by the credit mechanism. With the growth of credit, there develops a division between money as means of circulation and means of payment. During accumulation, credit serves the first function, so that commodities circulate on the promise of future payment. This development adds a further dimension to the metamorphosis of commodities, allowing for their circulation but moving their realization as money to the future.[45] This creates the possibility that at some future point the demand for the money commodity will exceed the demand for all other commodities to an extreme degree.[46] Were the pyramid of debt to be called in generally, an amount of money would be required to realize not only all currently produced commodities but also all those previously circulated by credit.

The pyramiding of credit, which facilitates the centralization of capital, is the financial side of the development of the productive forces. The development of the productive forces creates a quantitative difference between the value of commodities at the outset of the circuit of capital and at the moment of realization. As we have seen, this quantitative difference can turn the tendency of the rate of profit to fall into *actual* decline. With this actual decline, some capitals will no

[45] "The crisis in its second form is the function of money as means of payment, in which money has two different functions and figures in two different phases, divided from each other in time." *Ibid.*, II, p. 510.

[46] "At a given moment, the supply of all commodities can be greater than the demand for all commodities, since the demand for the *general commodity*, money, exchange value, is greater than the demand for all particular commodities; in other words the motive to turn the commodity into money, to realize its exchange value, prevails over the motive to transform the commodity into use value." *Ibid.*, II, p. 507.

longer be able to meet their debt obligations and will collapse financially. If sufficient capitals are so affected, a general credit crisis results, as described in Chapter V. This general credit crisis signals the beginning of a crisis of realization, so that commodities in general go unsold. It must be noted that the credit crises, like the fall in the rate of industrial profit, are activated by the interaction of capitals and cannot be analyzed or theoretically established at the level of capital-as-a-whole. Further, the interaction of capitals is not an interaction of equals, but an interaction of the strong and the weak, of the more efficient and the less efficient. In general, the less efficient capitals will suffer more in the credit crisis. But the larger, more efficient capitals will also be threatened with financial collapse, since they, too, have entered into credit buying; indeed, it is through growing indebtedness that the more efficient capitals have become more efficient. In order to install new means of production, the more efficient capitals have used the credit system to centralize capital in their hands. The credit collapse imposes itself upon both the strong and the weak and all in between.

We can summarize the process of accumulation and crisis as follows. The necessity to realize commodities as money creates the possibility of capitalist crisis, a possibility historically specific, predicated upon general commodity production, itself created by labor power being a commodity. The particular form of capitalist crisis derives from the division between money as means of circulation and as a means of payment, which creates a structure of growing indebtedness. This is not merely an institutional division, but a necessary division in order to restructure the division of labor. The cause of capitalist crisis is the tendency of the rate of profit to fall, a tendency arising from the sphere of production. This tendency finds expression through the formation of new values, through the interaction of capitals (competition). A fall in the rate of profit is the qualitative change that activates the developing tensions in the accumulation process. First, it implies a slowdown in accumulation, since there becomes relatively less surplus value to convert into new

capital. Second, it bankrupts inefficient capitals, setting off
a credit collapse. The resultant inability to realize value, because all commodities cannot be sold or not at their values,
is the crisis itself.

Marx summarized in similar terms,

> The general *possibility* of crisis is given in the process of
> metamorphosis of capital itself, and in two ways: in so
> far as money functions as *means of circulation*, [the pos-
> sibility of crisis lies in] the separation *of purchase and sale*;
> and in so far as money functions as *means of payment*, it
> has two different aspects, it acts as *measure of value* and
> as *realization of value*. These two aspects [may] become
> separated. If *in the interval* between them the value has
> changed, if the commodity at the moment of its sale is
> not *worth* what it was *worth* at the moment when money
> was acting as a measure of value and therefore as a
> measure of reciprocal obligation, then the obligation
> cannot be met from the *proceeds of the sale of the commod-
> ity* . . .
>
> . . .
>
> . . . [I]t is quite clear, that between the starting-point,
> the prerequisite capital, and the time of its return at the
> end of one of the periods, great catastrophes must occur
> and elements of crises must have gathered and devel-
> oped.[47]

Crucial here are the dynamics of the accumulation process,
the fact that time intervenes between the two moments of
circulation (M-C and C'-M'), an interval of production. This
necessary separation involves a change in values between the
two moments of circulation, and as a result, "elements of
crises must have gathered and developed." The crisis itself,
as we have seen in our discussion of credit, can lead to a
general fall in the exchange value of commodities as all commodities cannot be realized. Most important here is the

---

[47] *Ibid.*, pp. 513-514, 495. The emphasis and first two bracketed inserts
are in the text.

"moral depreciation" of existing means of production. Insofar as existing means of production are not materially destroyed through enforced idleness, it is their value which is affected. Bankrupt capitals liquidate their material assets, selling out to the surviving, more efficient capitals. Some of this socially obsolete means of production has been devalued. This devaluation itself raises the rate of profit on obsolete means of production and extends their useful life as part of the value-producing process.

The crisis was caused by the fall in the rate of profit, resulting from the implicit devaluation of means of production by technical change. In the crisis, the devaluation becomes explicit. Old means of production are forced to circulate in their entirety as the result of financial failures, i.e., to be sold off. What was latent during accumulating—the inability to realize fixed capital at its original value—becomes an actual failure when these means of production are liquidated in order to meet credit obligations.[48] This collapse of capital values momentarily resolves the contradictions in the process of value formation, laying the basis for a higher rate of profit and renewed accumulation.[49]

In Chapter V we argued that in a credit crisis, the preservation of the financial value of fictitious capital is preserved by the devaluation of commodities, which increases the value of money. Part of this process is the devaluation of the means of production, forcing the circulation of their value, part of which remained "fixated" in the period of expansion.

---

[48] "The specific feature about [capitalist accumulation] is that it uses the existing value of capital as a means of increasing this value to the utmost. The methods by which it accomplishes this include the fall of the rate of profit, depreciation of existing capital, and the development of the productive forces of labor at the expense of already created productive forces." *Capital*, III, p. 249.

[49] "The periodic depreciation of existing capital—one of the means immanent in capitalist production to check the fall of the rate of profit and hasten accumulation of capital-value through formation of new capital—disturbs the given conditions, within which the process of circulation and reproduction takes place, and is therefore accompanied by sudden stoppages and crises in the production process." *Ibid.*, p. 249.

The economic crisis in its full development, therefore, involves the devaluation of capital on the one hand achieved on the other by the growing idleness of the proletariat.[50]

In the crisis, the process of devaluation converts the organic composition of capital into the value composition. That is, the process of value formation, which proceeds by incremental steps during accumulation, is sharply accelerated during the crisis, and values rapidly approach the level implied by the most advanced forces of production that are in use. The process of accumulation is, as we have seen, a process of dynamic uneven development, during which technical change repeatedly lays the basis for new sets of values. This uneven development generates its own compensating force, the economic crisis. During the crisis, socially obsolete means of production are physically discarded and socially devalued. The new values latent in the new productive forces emerge to rule exchange. As a consequence, the valorized composition of capital may fall (CC/VC) and the rate of surplus value rise (SV/VC), the latter occurring as a result of a fall in the value of the commodities workers normally consume. A new and higher rate of profit is established (given the standard of living) by the combination of devalued fixed capital (in the denominator of the profit formula) and a rise in the rate of surplus value (in the numerator).

G. The "Inevitability" of Crises and the Development of Capitalism

The elements giving rise to economic crises are inherent in the accumulation process. Specifically, capitalism is a mode of production that generates repeated revolutions in the

---

[50] "[A] sudden general increase in the forces of production would relatively devalue all the *present values* which labor objectifies at the lower stage of the productive forces, and hence would destroy present capital as well as present laboring capacity. The other side of the crisis resolves itself into a real decrease in production, in living labor—in order to restore the correct relation between necessary and surplus labor, on which, in the last analysis, everything rests." *Grundrisse*, p. 446.

forces of production. This dynamic characteristic of the mode of production itself sets the limits to accumulation, since the development of the productive forces undermines the basis upon which surplus value is realized at any moment. As a consequence, crises are inherent in accumulation, since accumulation is the process of the revolutionizing of the means of production.

But also inherent in the process of capitalist reproduction is the recovery from crises. The same process that makes crisis necessary also provides for recovery, renewed accumulation. Thus from the process of accumulation itself there is no reason to predict or expect a final crisis that because of its severity will for economic reasons alone result in the collapse of the capitalist system and the automatic emergence of socialist society. This conclusion was clearly recognized by Lenin, and because of it, he argued that the end of capitalism in any country would come as a violent political confrontation between the bourgeoisie and the proletariat.

Crises result, as we have seen, from the uneven development of capital. Capitalism is the first mode of production in which revolutions in the forces of production are inherent in social reproduction. This is because social reproduction for capital-as-a-whole is the process of accumulation. However, these revolutions in production occur in the context of the anarchy of capitalist production, creating the stratification of capitals in terms of efficient use of the productive forces. As accumulation proceeds, the structure of capital as many capitals becomes increasingly fragile, and the reproduction of capital-as-a-whole is blocked by the antagonistic interaction of many capitals; capital-as-a-whole comes into conflict with the mutual interaction of its decentralized parts.

The crises generated by this conflict partially resolve the conflict, as a portion of capital is sacrificed for the well-being of capital-as-a-whole. Inefficient capitals are eliminated, either dropping out of existence altogether or by being absorbed by other capitals. This lays the basis for further accumulation upon a firmer basis. Thus, crises are both a devastating shock and the means to further accumulation. They are "inevitable" in that accumulation and its accompanying technical change are inherent in capitalist reproduction. They are also a moment of renewal. Perhaps the most grotesque and irrational aspect of capital's inner nature is that periods of deprivation for the masses of the population provide the mechanism to re-energize capital. Out of the ashes of unemployment, unsold commodities and idle productive forces, capital arises to repeat the accumulation-crisis cycle.

But this cyclical repetition does not proceed in mere duplication. The development of capitalism is contradictory, in that social relations change in such a way as both to facilitate and to block the rejuvenative effects of crises. On the positive side, from the point of view of capital's reproduction, the credit system grows more sophisticated, making the centralization of capital easier. State direct action grows, providing a lever to centralize and reorganize capital without the devastating discipline of economic collapse. Both the development of the credit system and action by the state, however, are predicated upon and increase the centralization of capital, so that each cycle of accumulation and crisis occurs in the context of social system dominated by larger and more powerful capitals. As matters proceed, the point is reached where the inefficient capitals to be eliminated in the reorganization called forth by crises are not small and weak and inefficient, but large and powerful and inefficient. Examples of this abound—British Leyland and Rolls-Royce in the United Kingdom, Chrysler and U.S. Steel in the United States. It is clear that such powerful economic institutions cannot be restructured or eliminated by economic processes alone. In the epoch of monopoly capitalism, capitalist production becomes controlled by immense financial institutions that can invoke the aid of the state to prevent their disintegration in face of competitive pressures. As a consequence, the function of economic crises is undermined, and the necessary attrition of the inefficient capitals is blocked.

State action to reduce the severity of crises cannot but have contradictory results. The uneven development of capital creates the conditions for the tendency of the rate of profit to fall, and the tendency via the credit system produces financial or monetary crises, followed by crises of generalized overproduction. The state can act to maintain demand, using Keynesian monetary and fiscal policy, and this can postpone the crisis of realization. However, this is done at the cost of maintaining a fragile structure of stratified capitals. Postponing a crisis of realization prevents the devaluation of fixed capital that would facilitate the reorganization of capital. This is precisely what occurred in the United States economy in the postwar period, and also in the United Kingdom. As a consequence, a burden of inefficiency was carried forward, and by the 1960s, U.S. capital was being undersold in foreign markets; by the 1970s, U.S. capital could not maintain its control over domestic markets in major commodities such as steel, consumer electronics, and automobiles. As disruptive and devastating as crises may be for capitalists, the long term consequences of "controlling" the business cycle are even more catastrophic. U.S. capital has reached the point where accumulation can be sustained only in the context of growing foreign competition in domestic markets and powerful inflationary pressures.

The law of value is the law of value formation, and its necessary elements—the value form, money form, credit, competition, and revolutions in the means of production—generate uneven development of capital that somehow must be resolved. As the role of the state grows and competition is increasingly among giant capitals, the severity of a crisis that would be able to affect a significant restructuring of capital grows. The alternative to such a crisis in a world of national capitalist states is the economic decline of some national capitals, which taken as a whole fall behind in the revolutionizing of the means of production. Capital-as-a-whole requires periodic restructuring, and in its reproduction provides the means to this restructuring, crisis; capital as many capitals resists this means. This basic contradiction, which intensifies as capitalism develops, is essentially unresolvable.

Marx wrote that, in each mode of production, the development of the productive forces reaches a point where the social relations governing production and distribution come in conflict with the further development of those productive forces. The advanced capitalist countries have reached that point. The social relations that two hundred years ago liberated the productive forces for a great burst of development now serve to restrict that development, ushering in an era in which the tensions accompanying accumulation lay the basis for the possibility of a revolutionary transformation of capitalist society; but only the possibility. The transformation will not occur automatically; it will require a consciously directed class struggle to overthrow bourgeois rule.

INDEX

LIBRARY OF CONGRESS CATALOGING IN PUBLICATION DATA

Weeks, John, 1941-
  Capital and exploitation.

  Includes bibliographical references and index.
  1. Capitalism.   2. Value.   3. Marxian
economics.   I. Title.
HB501.W472   335.4'12   81-47163
ISBN 0-691-04228-4   AACR2
ISBN 0-691-00366-1 (pbk.)